Praise for *Is Your Genius at Work?*

"Brilliant, accessible, and fun! A 'must read' for career consultants, counselors, and coaches, and invaluable for anyone who wants to help people embrace their unique potential."

**John R. Landgraf, pastoral counselor and career counselor;
author, *Singling: A New Way to Live the Single Life***

"I have embraced the concepts Dick Richards articulates in my personal life and in my leadership coaching practice. The most striking result I have seen in myself and others is the emergence of a powerful sense of inner peace as we finally know how to align what we do with who we are and why we are here."

**Michael W. Wold, principal consultant and leadership coach,
TeamWorks International, Inc.**

"I've found it easier to relate to clients and friends having named my genius. And, I find it's a useful tool to offer to people so that they know how to best utilize my skills."

Roy Blumenthal, artist-at-large

"Goosebumps! That's what I felt when the name of my genius found me, using the tools outlined in this book. Even several years later, my development personally and professionally continues to evolve from naming my genius."

**Debbie Call, principal, Moving Spirit, LLC; coach; author,
*Tug of Heart: How to Trust What You Know***

"Dick Richards is a genius! With clarity and insight, he guides any willing reader through a process of revelation. By connecting with my genius, I added a spark of passion and enthusiasm for my calling that I did not have before."

Michele Whittington, senior minister, Creative Living Fellowship

"The beauty of Dick Richards' approach is its simplicity; however, the results are anything but simple. Just knowing that you are working with your genius will create certainty and clarity of purpose."

Geoffrey Lory, project coach; columnist, ProjectConnections.com

"Reader-friendly, packs a terrific punch, and customized for the workplace. It will be a boon to my consulting practice as well as to my life."

Allen Zaklad, Ph.D., president, Allen Zaklad Associates

"Gives us a way to navigate even if all around us is chaos. This book helps us take charge of our work, our lives, and ourselves."

Christine Moore, consultant and coach, Arthur Maxwell

"Dick Richards has discovered some profound, life-changing concepts and maps out a practical path for putting them into practice. He has clearly put his genius to work in creating this masterpiece."

Marvin Israelow, career development consultant

"Provides a practical and insightful approach for discovering your unique genius. This is invaluable information for anyone seeking a truly inspired life."

Dianna Anderson, MCC, coauthor, *Coaching That Counts*

"Refreshing, deep, insightful, and practical. Buy this book, read it, and use it as a frequent reference."

Linne Bourget, founder & CEO, Institute for Transformation Leaders & Consultants; author, *What You Say Is What You Get*™

"Dick Richards' book transformed my life. I successfully took these exercises and created a workshop for groups of people in recovery locally, regionally, and nationally."

Sarah Munro, coordinator, Central Vermont Compassionate Community Collaborative

"Discovering my genius was the catalyst for me to leave corporate America, launch my business, and live a fulfilling life. Since 1997, I have used Dick Richards' genius concepts as a primary filter for successfully staying on purpose and guiding others to do the same."

Barbara K. Simasko, principal, Omega Coaching Group, Inc.

"I started my path to finding my genius when I came across Dick Richards' first book. About a year later, I was in a session with Dick finding my genius. Many life experiences since then have reinforced my genius, and knowing it has helped me make better life decisions."

Jesse Freese, president & CEO, Fissure Corporation

IS YOUR GENIUS AT WORK?

IS YOUR GENIUS AT WORK?

4 KEY QUESTIONS TO ASK
BEFORE YOUR NEXT CAREER MOVE

DICK RICHARDS

Davies-Black Publishing
Mountain View, California

Published by Davies-Black Publishing, a division of CPP, Inc., 1055 Joaquin Road, 2nd Floor, Mountain View, CA 94043; 800-624-1765.

Special discounts on bulk quantities of Davies-Black books are available to corporations, professional associations, and other organizations. For details, contact the Director of Marketing and Sales at Davies-Black Publishing: 650-691-9123; fax 650-623-9271.

Visit the Davies-Black Publishing Web site at www.daviesblack.com.

Printed in the United States of America.
11   10   09   08   07   10   9   8   7   6   5   4   3   2

Library of Congress Cataloging-in-Publication Data
Richards, Dick
     Is your genius at work? : four key questions to ask before your next career
     move / Dick Richards.—1st ed.
          p. cm.
     Includes bibliographical references and index.
     ISBN 978-0-89106-194-6 (pbk.)
     1. Self-actualization (Psychology) 2. Self-perception. 3. Success—
          Psychological aspects. 4. Genius. I. Title.
     BF637.S4R49 2005
     158.7—dc22
                                                                        2005024561
FIRST EDITION
First printing 2005

*To every person who has shared
his or her genius with me*

CONTENTS

EXERCISES

PREFACE

At about age seven, I was sitting on a bench in front of a hardware store on Germantown Avenue in Philadelphia, waiting for my father to emerge with whatever gizmo he had gone into the store to buy. This was in the 1950s, when streets were swept by hand. A man in baggy gray trousers and a flat cap was pushing a broom along the cobblestone street. The area in front of him was littered with fall leaves. The area behind him was as clean as any cobblestone street can be. He pushed his broom with ease.

I don't remember what I thought as I watched, but I do recall a sense that was something like wonder. It was the kind of feeling that visits us when we look at something brilliant, similar to the feeling I had the first time I saw the Eiffel Tower or watched the beginning of the first World Series game I attended.

I like to think this book was conceived at that moment, when I wondered at the brilliance and ease of the man's street sweeping. For as long as I can recall, I have known that the brilliance and ease of a person's work have little to do with the nature of the work itself. I have seen and known brilliant managers, farmers, tire changers, electricians and plumbers, executives, customer service representatives, coaches and therapists, entertainers, salespeople, artists, teachers, and so on.

This book is for anyone who needs a change in his or her work. It is about what I believe to be the main differences between people who do their work with brilliance and ease and those who do not. The former, through either design, luck, or fate, bring their natural power and energy to their work. I call that natural power and energy *genius*. They also bring to their work a sense that it contributes somehow to something larger than themselves. I call that sense *purpose*.

If you want your work and career to resonate with your natural power and your purpose, you need to find a match between what is **out there** in the world of possibility and what is **with you**. Your genius is at the core of what is with you. I hope to help you understand that core.

Recent surveys showing that significant numbers of people are dissatisfied with their jobs provided much of the stimulus for this book. If you are one of those people, matching what is out there with what is with you is critical to achieving a happier and more productive work life. The world of possibility—out there—is transparent. An Internet search turned up 47.5 million hits for the word *career*. Those hits included career centers, career services, bulletin boards, and advice—coaching, planning, publications, and tests—as well as information about careers for women and careers in technology, business, education, marketing, service, and so forth. We have much more information and advice about possibilities, and how to pitch our experience and talents, than familiarity with those deep aspects of ourselves that seek fulfillment through work.

Because the world of possibility is transparent, we can find what is out there without much effort. The more difficult task is determining what is with you. This book makes that task easier.

Since the early 1980s, I have been on the trail of genius, trying to understand what it is and developing techniques to help others recognize it in themselves. Chapters 1 through 6 contain the understanding. Notations within the chapters alert you to related exercises, grouped in a separate section, that fit the chapter text. In recent years, many fine thinkers have offered us a blizzard of material about purpose in the form of books, audiotapes and videotapes, workshops, and television programs. I have focused on helping you recognize your genius in this book and, for the most part, tried to avoid repeating what others have already said. But because genius and purpose are so tightly linked, Chapter 7 contains a summary of how modern thinkers have approached the question of purpose and offers suggestions on detecting yours. And finally, Chapter 8 provides guidance on keeping yourself in tune, so that the energy of your genius remains focused on your purpose in life and at work.

The stories in this book come from my experiences with real people or are based on what they reported to me. Some of them prefer to remain anonymous, so, with the exception of Michael Azzopardi, I used only fictitious first names. I also occasionally altered inconsequential details about different people.

In these pages, I invite you to examine your work from a perspective that you probably have not used before. This perspective takes into account both your genius and your purpose and offers the possibility that you will find the work that you can do with brilliance and ease. Within that work, you are most likely to find success and satisfaction.

ACKNOWLEDGMENTS

It takes more than an author to create a book. It also takes inspiration, and then production. So I offer thanks to Calvin Germain and Marvin Israelow, for the inspiration that set this book on its course, and to my literary agent, John Willig, and my editor at Davies-Black, Connie Kallback, both of whom summoned the faith that launched it into production.

Many hundreds of people have shared their stories with me, either in personal coaching and counseling sessions or in workshops. The stories of some are told here, but the stories of all those people contributed to the understanding that fills these pages. I am grateful to every one of them.

Thanks also to these people in particular, some of whom told their stories, helped me find people who told stories, or otherwise provided me with much needed help, encouragement, and feedback: Linne Bourget, Debbie Call, Joyce Filupeit, Jesse Freese, Nick Head, Geof Lory, Christine Moore, Sarah Munro, Cheryl Stumbo, Toni Webster, Jim Wold, Mike Wold, and Allen Zaklad.

Finally, there are two people to whom I want to offer special gratitude. George Davis has contributed to my life, my work, and this book in myriad invaluable ways. My wife, Melanie, has been editor, inspiration, voice of integrity, and champion for this book and is my *anam cara*.

ABOUT THE AUTHOR

Dick Richards draws on his rich coaching, speaking, and consulting experience, his considerable skill at getting to the heart of the matter, and his faith in the human spirit to help people and organizations achieve their aspirations. He has worked with more than fifty organizations of all sizes and in more than a dozen countries—in business, social service, health care, and education—developing and leading programs to improve leadership, career development, teamwork, and customer service and to implement strategy.

Richards has been on the leading edge of efforts to bring feeling and spirit to workplaces since the publication of his first book, *Artful Work: Awakening Joy, Meaning, and Commitment in the Workplace*, which won a Benjamin Franklin Award as Best Business Book. He was among the 150 world-renowned business thought leaders and practitioners commissioned to provide essays for *Business: The Ultimate Resource*, the landmark reference work on business and management. He frequently writes about leadership, customer service, change, and life-work for professional and Internet publications and is also the author of *The Art of Winning Commitment: 10 Ways Leaders Can Engage Minds, Hearts, and Spirits*.

Three of Richards' gifts, as described by clients of his coaching and change consulting practice, are his ability to "talk hard about the soft stuff," to create "an unusually effective combination of heart and mind, coupled with business sophistication and a results focus," and to be "one of the world's best listeners."

Richards and his wife, Melanie, live in Phoenix, Arizona. Visit his Web site at **www.ongenius.com**.

Answer Four Key Questions

The forms of all things are derived from their genius.
—WILLIAM BLAKE

YOU HAVE A GENIUS that is inevitably linked to your work and career. Everyone does. And each person's genius is unique. Your genius can be thought of in a practical way: as the exceptional power that comes most naturally to you, as the process you undertake so spontaneously and easily that you do not notice it, and as the business in which you are engaged as a person. It can also be thought of in a mystical way: as the energy of your soul and as an answer to the question of why you exist within the human community. Your genius has been a source of success and satisfaction in work that you have done in the past, and it will be the source of success and satisfaction in your future work. It is a major factor in determining why some situations feel just right, while others feel just awful.

For more than twenty years, I have been helping people recognize their geniuses, through counseling and coaching relationships; personal development, career development, leadership, and management-training workshops; and team-building processes. Over those years, I developed strategies and exercises to enable people to recognize themselves at a very deep level: the level of their own geniuses. The strategies and exercises, as well as the experience of guiding people toward recognizing their geniuses, form the core of this book.

Having done this work over such a long period, I was able to revisit people who have long recognized their geniuses and ask them, "So what? What difference has that recognition meant to you?" Their answers validate the idea that recognizing your genius can be a turning point in your life. An information technology consultant described it as life changing. A business consultant told me that she reframed her business, rewrote her corporate mission statement, renamed her company, and redesigned her Web site after recognizing her genius. A man who had recently begun a job search said that understanding his genius helped him explain the unique contribution he could make to prospective employers. The CEO of a sales-training company observed that recognizing his genius had helped him understand not only his successes but also his failures and avoid situations that were likely to fail. A project manager said, about both his work and his parenting, "It all flows back to my genius." A marketing executive made a career change and is happy and thriving.

The people I spoke with often used the word *profound* to describe the experience of recognizing their geniuses and the effect that recognition has had on them. One of them said, "It was as if a celestial being of some sort looked over my shoulder and said, 'It is good.' I felt a powerful release from the unrealistic expectations of others—and of myself. Expectations that had not a prayer of becoming real but had the potential to be thought of as nagging shortcomings and disappointments."

To summarize what I know from my own experience, and from what I have heard from other people, there are at least six significant advantages to recognizing your genius.

First, you gain a **stronger sense of identity.** Recognizing your genius provides you with a positive perception of yourself at a deeper and more meaningful level than the sense generated by other self-assessment and self-awareness techniques. One person commented, "At the moment of naming my genius, my life was slammed into focus. What had been fuzzy, or had danced at the edge of consciousness, became clear. I instantly understood why I do what I do. I instantly understood why I don't do what I don't do. Most important, it made it OK that I do what I do and not what I don't."

Second, recognizing your genius grants you a **clearer sense of direction**. It helps you understand that some situations will be ideal for you, while others will not. It helps you distinguish between the things that others have taught you that you should do, but that are not consistent with who you are, and the things that are consistent with who you are. When coupled with a sense of mission, recognizing your genius offers a glimpse, and perhaps a blinding flash, about the course your life must take in the future.

Third, those who have recognized their geniuses often report that they feel **increased confidence.** The deep self-knowledge that comes from recognizing your genius helps you know when you are on exactly the right track and to understand when you have within yourself exactly what is needed to reach your goals. When people have that knowledge, they seem to "catch fire," to go about their work with renewed passion and determination.

Fourth, when you recognize your genius, you will also have the **language to communicate the value you can add** to the opportunities you pursue. People who come to recognize their geniuses are able to convey more easily to others who they are, what they do best, how and why they do what they do, and what they need in order to achieve success. This ability is invaluable when job seeking, deciding if a particular type of work is right for you, or explaining to clients how you can help them.

Fifth, you are likely to experience **satisfaction and productivity in your work** when you recognize your genius and choose work that engages it. Your genius has been involved during those periods when things seemed to flow, when you lost track of time and felt fully engaged in whatever you were doing. Since the energy of your genius comes easily and spontaneously, you quite naturally enjoy it.

A man who has known his genius for about eight years said, "I've been able to change my work so that it's more congruous with my genius. But there's more. I not only feel more satisfaction; I actually get more done. I'm more productive. I devote myself to the work of my genius rather than frittering it away trying to do what I cannot do; I'm doing what I'm good at instead of breaking my neck trying to fix imagined deficiencies."

Finally, there is a **sense of personal harmony** that arises when your genius is aligned with your everyday activities. One man said about recognizing his genius, "This knowledge provides a kind of inner peace. It's hard to describe the feeling, but when I get up in the morning and engage people, I have a compass that guides me. And when I'm in my genius zone, I feel at peace. I'm home."

FOUR KEY QUESTIONS

The first step toward recognizing your genius is acknowledging that you do have a genius. The idea may seem surprising or quite foreign, yet it is an ancient one that has become impoverished in our culture. We tend to think of genius as a mental capacity, a number on an IQ test, or a quality attached only to those who achieve extraordinary creative accomplishments. The idea is much more fertile than that and has been alive in many cultures throughout many ages.

Today, we are more likely to agonize over our apparent shortcomings and failures than to recognize something unique and valuable about ourselves. In the time we take for self-reflection, we are usually busy asking what is wrong with us. "Why can't I be more myself?" "How did my family contribute to my dysfunction?" "Why can't I commit to a relationship?" "Why can't I find satisfying work?" While it may be fruitful to shine the light of awareness on our problems and flaws, it is equally fruitful to bring our unique gifts out of the darkness. Your genius is one of your gifts.

If you have doubts that you do have a genius, I urge you to suspend those doubts and continue reading.

When you acknowledge that you have a genius, even if you do not understand its unique qualities, you will be better able to respond to four questions, and your answers can deliver invaluable guidance about your work and career. The initial question must be answered first because it is the foundation for answering the others.

1. What is your genius?

Once you acknowledge that you do or may have a genius, the next step is to recognize its unique qualities. The following five chapters will help you do that.

2. Is your genius at work?

This question has two meanings: Is your genius working in the way that it should? and Can you bring your genius to whatever work you are doing? When you have recognized your genius, you will know whether the work you are doing engages your genius sufficiently to provide success and satisfaction for you, whether and how it is possible for you to gain success and satisfaction where you are, whether a change would be better for you, and what kind of change that might be.

3. What is your purpose?

Your purpose is a specific external expression of your genius. It is the earthly reason your genius exists. The concept of a purpose that provides direction for our lives has, like the concept of genius, been with us since ancient times and has existed in many variations and in many cultures. Unlike the idea of genius, however, it has become less clouded over time and has been addressed by many contemporary thinkers.

4. Is your genius on purpose?

Satisfaction, productivity, and success in your work arise to the extent that the work allows you to bring the energy of your genius to the fulfillment of your life's purpose.

In the diagram below, I use the term *self* to refer to the characteristics that make up the physical and psychological you. The diagram shows the self in its ideal form, as the perfect means by which your genius may act on your purpose within the context of your life and work. Your self, however, could either nurture or hamper your genius. For example, fear of failure hampers your genius by causing you to avoid needed action, while a more fearless attitude allows you to take necessary risks.

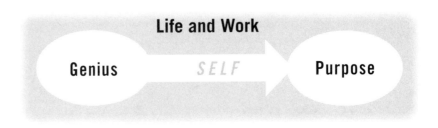

The shaded area of the diagram represents your life and work, which, like your self, either nurtures or hampers your genius and purpose. Your life and work together form the context within which your genius, self, and purpose come alive.

ENGAGING THE HEART

The story of Francine and her genius illustrates the central importance of the first key question and shows how answering that question suggests answers to the others. Her story also conveys an overview of the concept of genius, a taste of the process that you must carry out in order to recognize your own genius, and a look into the relationship between genius and work.

Francine asked me to meet with her because an important decision about her work was brewing, and she wanted to sort out her thoughts and feelings. In a telephone conversation a few days before our meeting, I suggested that it would be useful to explore her genius.

Francine and I are colleagues and friends, and she already had a cursory understanding of the term *genius*. She also understood that her best chance for success and satisfaction is through work that engages her genius. Francine, feeling neither successful nor satisfied in her job, agreed that exploring her genius would be useful. We met over lunch on a sunny patio overlooking the Ohio River, and she told me why she thought she might need a change of jobs.

At the time, Francine was employed as a psychologist by a large corporation. Her job involved helping the company's managers to develop themselves, their people, and the work environment. On the surface, the job seemed perfect for her because she had devoted her career to helping other people grow in their understanding of themselves. But intellect and logic reigned in the company's culture, while emotion and hunches were suspect.

In her most recent performance appraisal, her boss had admonished her for crying during a meeting in which plans were made for a large downsizing. She explained to me that she felt sadness, because many people would have their lives overturned, as well as a sense of failure, because the company was not profitable enough to provide security for its people. Her show of feelings was disruptive, her boss had insisted. In his view, although the choice to downsize was difficult, it was, after all, the logical thing to do—the only thing to do. So she should have put her feelings aside.

Francine believed that although the decision to downsize was logical and right, sadness and acknowledgment that the act would cause pain were psychologically healthy ways of dealing with the situation. She was discouraged from offering to help those who were staying with the company deal with their feelings about the decision, the absence of friends and colleagues, and their own survivor guilt. It was not only Francine who was being asked to put feelings aside—everyone in the company was expected to do so. To

Francine, this work environment seemed detrimental, not because the company was downsizing or because profits were low, but because her feelings about the situation were judged disruptive.

She said, "I'm angry at myself. When I first went into this, I was not fully aware of what I was in for. I keep thinking I should do something better, but I don't know what to do. I get irritated with myself, then mad at everybody else. I have a great deal of anger that is deadly to express in that climate. So I hold it in and beat myself up a lot."

She sat back in her chair, arms folded tightly across her body. She told me about a presentation she had attended the previous day. The presenter showed an audience of managers a chart containing columns of figures. Several people immediately began tapping away at their calculators, checking the addition in the chart.

"They were more interested in whether the addition was correct than in what the numbers meant," she said. "And they love to catch mistakes. They love to one-up another person."

Francine usually accepts and often values the differences between herself and others, and she is not prone to criticizing other people. But on that day, her posture and tone of voice made it clear that she was repelled by the climate of evaluation, analysis, and intellectual superiority. Her repulsion was a clue to her genius. We often find the behavior and attitudes of others repellent when they give offense to our genius. Francine's unspoken question—"How could they possibly be like that?"—suggested that her genius functions in the opposite direction from analysis and evaluation.

I asked her to clarify the difference between herself and those around her at work.

She unfolded her arms, leaned forward, and said, "I have to get right down to what matters, to the heart of things and to the heart of each person I work with. When my heart is engaged, I know that something is good and right and has to be done. This is not an intellectual knowing, and it's not exactly a feeling. It's a deep inner knowledge."

As she spoke, her hands came alive in waves and flutters. Her attitude changed. She talked about getting to the heart of things with conviction and pride. Her eyes were alight.

I was listening to her in a special way, listening to the content of what she was saying and also for clues to her genius. Those clues are most often found in posture, gestures, tone of voice, emphasis, repetition, and choice of words. In this last declaration, Francine said "heart" three times, each time with more energy.

There is a firm rule about helping someone to recognize his or her genius, and this rule stipulates that the person is the only expert on his or her genius. I may offer guesses, observations, experience, and this special kind of listening, but the person, in this case, Francine, is the only authority, the only one who can really know.

I made a guess based on what I saw and what she had told me so far. Her heart must be involved in what she does, and she was frustrated that those around her seemed not to have their hearts involved, only their minds. Your frustration is another clue to your genius. You will feel frustrated when your genius is thwarted by the circumstances or people around you.

I said, "It sounds like your genius has something to do with bringing the heart into play. Is your genius Involving the Heart?"

The primary method for recognizing your genius is finding a name for it, like the one I proposed to Francine. The next few chapters will help you find the right name for your genius.

"The right word is not *involving*," she said. "The heart is always involved. But it's not always *engaged*."

One of the more satisfying aspects of helping someone recognize his or her genius is that I don't have to be right when I guess, only close, and the person will refine what I have offered. In fact, I am in danger of subverting the other person's process if I maintain that I am right.

Francine was thoughtful for a moment and then said, "My genius isn't Involving the Heart. It's Engaging the Heart."

Appendix A contains guidelines for people (such as coaches, counselors, etc.) who want to help a person recognize his or her genius (see page 171).

I was not sure how Francine distinguished between *involving* and *engaging*, but it doesn't matter if I understand. It only matters that she does.

After she said this—"Engaging the Heart"—she sat back again, her hands resting on the table, looking directly at me. There was a long moment of silence as she took in what she had just said, followed by a smile and a sigh of recognition. This is an important moment, this moment of recognizing your genius.

She said, "I had to learn the logical stuff that's so important to the people I work with, and I'm good at it. I know I'm smart; I have all the degrees to prove it. But I can't exist in that rational, logical framework all the time. There's more to life than being intellectually adept."

Francine's education had taught her about engaging the mind, but she did not have to learn about engaging the heart. It is her genius, which comes to her naturally and spontaneously. It is an aspect of herself that she values but had not fully recognized or appreciated. It is hard to imagine an organizational climate more antithetical to Francine's genius than the one in which she worked; she is all heart and affirmation, while the people around her were all intellect and analysis. Her experience as an employee of the company frustrated her because she believed that she was not able to "get down to what really matters" with most of the people around her

Plaintively, she asked, "How do you measure the human spirit? How do you measure what is in the human heart? It certainly can't be done with a calculator."

Francine told me that she was going to leave the company. Until that moment, she had not been certain whether or why she had to leave. She had only believed it might be best, and so she had waffled. The reasons for leaving her job became clear to her when she recognized her genius.

She said, "I'm going to search for work that engages my heart, that allows me to engage the hearts of others. And I want to work with people who are doing the same."

ANSWERS

During our conversation, Francine answered the four key questions. First, she recognized her genius, Engaging the Heart. Everything else flowed from that recognition. Her answer to the question "Is your genius at work?" was "yes," but her situation was complicated. While her genius was working in the way that it should (her own heart was clearly engaged in what she was doing), she could not bring it to her job without great cost—the pain of having her genius thwarted, rejected, and admonished. Francine was the all-too-common square peg in a round hole. She was angry with herself for not doing "something better" because she had not yet accepted and understood that she was different from those around her. In short, her genius was at work, but the cost was too high for her to bear.

Francine already had an answer to the question "What is your purpose?" before our conversation. She knew that her purpose had to do with creating productive workplaces that respect the human spirit. Although she had made a commitment to helping the company create such a workplace, and was acting in accordance with her own purpose, she was unable to maintain a positive attitude about her work, which consequently suffered.

This is an example of how your self might intervene to either facilitate or hinder your genius as it works to fulfill your purpose. Francine got in her own way when she failed to recognize from the beginning that her current situation was wrong for her, when she began berating herself and getting angry at those around her, and when she continually tried to fit her square self into the company's round hole. In order to get out of her own way, she would have to continue to recognize her genius, seek work that makes the best use of it and allows her to fulfill her purpose, and surround herself with people who value what she has to offer. She would have to be alert for the signs that indicate she is in the wrong place. She would have to try less to fit in and more to seek or create situations that fit who she is.

Your self also addresses the inevitable compromises that you must face when you try to satisfy all of your values, when you try, for example, to be both creative and secure or both wealthy and self-sacrificing. Francine's job was high paying. Would she have to compromise on her salary or lifestyle if she chose to work at engaging her heart and the hearts of others? In order to answer that question, she would have to explore job options.

Francine answered the question "Is your genius on purpose?" with "yes." The problems she was experiencing were not about bringing her genius to her purpose but about where she chose to do so.

A WAY OF UNDERSTANDING

Clearly, your genius has important implications for your work and career, as it did for Francine. Your situation may be quite different from hers. For example, you may be content in your job but experiencing the sense that there is something else—or something more—that you are expected or want to do. In any case, the imperative to find work and embark on a career that will allow you to express your genius is the same as it was for Francine. When you recognize your genius, you also may realize that your work situation requires change. This realization will probably not be news to you. More likely, recognizing your genius will give you a way of understanding something that you have sensed for some time.

It is also possible that, if your current situation works well for you, you will recognize why it does. You might also discover that minor changes, less dramatic than Francine's, will make an enormous difference to you. For example, Jerry, a chemical engineer, was disenchanted with his work in the research laboratory of a petrochemical company. He calls his genius Offering Solutions—somewhat of a pun on his work as a chemist. Jerry would love to help you do a crossword puzzle, discover the best route to a driving destination, or identify that strange new noise coming from your car's engine. Although his job did involve finding solutions to problems, there just wasn't enough of offering solutions to others. Finding a solution without handing it off to someone who would put the solution into practice wasn't enough to satisfy Jerry's genius.

After much discussion between Jerry and his boss, the company found a new role for Jerry. It had been considering the experiment of equipping a truck with a chemical lab. The truck would be on call for problems with oil-drilling rigs and other heavy equipment that might require lubricants custom mixed on the spot. The company assigned Jerry to the experiment, giving him an opportunity to offer solutions.

When you recognize your genius as well as Francine and Jerry do, you will be able to avoid work that is wrong for you. Better yet, you will also be prepared to actively seek work that is fulfilling, that enables you to be most effective and productive, and that allows you to make the contribution that only you can make.

THE ELUSIVE GENIUS

The process of recognizing your genius is not usually as simple or as quick as it was for Francine. Some people are able to recognize their geniuses almost immediately after hearing about the idea, but this is very rare. In two-day workshops, in which people explore their geniuses intensively, a third of the participants commonly leave without achieving a satisfactory sense of their geniuses. Recognition usually does come within a few days—often at an unexpected time and place. Many people benefit from letting the idea that they have a genius, and that they can name it, percolate within them for a while.

Genius is elusive because we generally do not consider that we have a genius at all, or we ignore it or are not used to thinking about it. It also is not quantifiable, and its uniqueness implies that it will not be found with any single questionnaire. Francine was able to name and recognize her genius rather quickly because she is practiced at self-examination and because she had a sense of the concept before our conversation.

Even if you think you already have the right name for your genius, read the following chapters and do the exercises. You will probably discover that you need to refine or completely alter the name you now think is right. There is no single magic formula for recognizing your genius, only general guidelines and approaches to help you reach the point at which your genius becomes obvious to you.

Recognize
Your Genius

*Take care with a name: let its sound
echo with delight in your soul.*

—THE MONKS OF NEW SKETE

THE PRIMARY METHOD for recognizing your genius is to give it a name. Naming things is a deep-seated human activity. We name our children, of course. And we also name our nations, our mountains and rivers, our pets and products. We playfully name our noteworthy objects (I once owned a Saab named Thor). We create nicknames for those close to us.

Naming a thing is a complex endeavor that carries significant thought and accountability: consider the turmoil parents often go through when naming a child. When we name something, we gain a sense of ownership over it. I use the term *ownership* not so much in the sense of possessing something but more in the sense of stewardship over or responsibility for it. But the distinction between possession and responsibility has been the subject of debate for centuries. In the biblical book of Genesis, Adam is given the task of naming the animals. This suggests to many people that God granted mastery over animals to Adam and his descendants, while others infer that Adam was given not mastery but responsibility.

When my wife and I named our dog, Gypsy, she became ours in a way that she had not been until then. In some spiritual traditions, when a person knows the name of a demon or a god, he or she can control it. In Judaism, only high priests are permitted to pronounce the name of God because daring to say the name suggests control over God.

Our names hold great power in and of themselves. They impart a sense of identity, an intimation to ourselves and to others of who we are, or who we can be expected to be. One expects a man named Marion to be different from a man named John. This is likely the reason that Marion Morrison became John Wayne.

We often acquire new titles after an important event, signifying that we are in some way different from the person we were before, becoming, for example, a Mrs. or a Dr. Important events are often accompanied by a personal transformation. Simon became Peter, Saul became Paul, Jacob became Israel, Cassius Clay became Muhammad Ali, and Lew Alcindor became Kareem Abdul-Jabbar. Native Americans receive new names to signify that their role, status, or wisdom has grown, or that they have somehow become new people.

Having a name for something also makes it seem more real and more accessible. Once, on a clear, bright winter morning, I watched from afar as a gust of wind blew a puff of snow from the peak of Mount Hood. The mere mention or thought of the name—Mount Hood—now conjures that image in my mind. This may be why we engrave the name of a deceased loved one on a stone marker. Is it not only to mark the spot but also to evoke the image of the person as we read the name?

Names are also important facets of relationship. We know someone in a more intimate way when we know that person's name. We feel differently, more connected to people whose names we know. And various levels of relationship are often reflected in the use of different names. "My name is Jim, but my friends call me Scooter" is as much a statement about relationship as it is about a name.

To name something after searching for just the right name means to "get it" in both senses of the term: to understand it and to own it. The act of naming your genius will give you that understanding and ownership. It will make your genius more real and accessible to you. It will also change your relationship to your genius, as you will have a connection with it that is both more knowing and more intimate. Finding the name of your genius is often transformative, but we must not forget that the name is not the thing named and that our experience of the thing we have named is far more complex than the name itself.

Plato, in his *Cratylus*, describes a dialogue between Socrates and Cratylus in which they discuss the how and why of naming things. Socrates doesn't care very much if the name of a thing indicates its nature. Cratylus, however, insists that the very reason for naming a thing is to reflect its nature. From his point of view, we must already know the thing before we can properly name it.[1]

For the purpose of naming your genius, we must agree with Cratylus—partly. You do want to find a name that reflects the nature of your genius; however, the process of naming it and that of knowing it will be the same.

THE FELT SENSE

Although finding a name for your genius is important, the more important outcome of the naming process is developing a felt sense of your genius. Finding a name is a device for developing that sense.

In his book *Focusing*, Eugene Gendlin describes a felt sense in this way:

> A felt sense is not a mental experience but a physical one. Physical.
> A bodily awareness of a situation or person or event. An internal aura
> that encompasses everything you feel and know about the given

subject at a given time—encompasses it and communicates it to you all at once rather than detail by detail. Think of it as a taste, if you like, or a great musical chord that makes you feel a powerful impact, a big round unclear feeling.[2]

A felt sense, according to Gendlin, has these characteristics:

- It is not a mere mental experience but an internal body awareness.
- It is almost always unclear at first.
- It arrives not in the form of thoughts or words or other separate units but as a single bodily feeling.
- It is not an emotion but has emotional components along with mental components.
- It has the power to create change.
- When you experience a felt sense, something in your body releases, something that felt tight, lets go.[3]

You will know that you have found the correct name to describe your genius when the arrival of the name in your mind is accompanied by the felt sense of its rightness. That arrival will correspond to the characteristics Gendlin describes. The moment when the right name and the "big round unclear feeling" appear often seems magical. Additional discussion and many examples are found in Chapter 6.

TRYING IT ON

During workshops that lead people to recognize their geniuses, organizers use name tags to keep track of each person's progress. Whenever a person believes that he or she has discovered the right name for a genius, that person writes the name on a name tag and wears it. People often go through a dozen name tags in the course of a few days.

If you have an idea of what your genius might be, write its name in the name tag here. Do not worry about being "right." Simply record your best guess at the moment. Name tags like this one will appear throughout this book. Each time you see one, write in the name that seems right to you at that time.

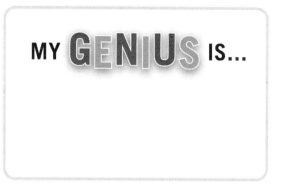

A THOUGHT EXPERIMENT

Giving a name to your genius is a thought experiment, a method for analyzing theories and solving problems by using the power of imagination. In philosophy, the history of thought experiments extends back in time at least to Plato, and in science, to Galileo. Thought experiments have been most alive in more recent times in the work of Albert Einstein and quantum physicists.

In order to perform a thought experiment, you must imagine that certain things are happening or are true and then examine the consequences of what you have imagined. For example, one of the best-known thought experiments is Einstein's "moving train" experiment. Einstein imagined two bolts of lightning striking as a train moves through a station. Viewers of the event see the sequence of lightning strikes differently depending on whether they are on the stationary platform or on the moving train at the time the event occurs. Einstein asked, "Which viewer is correct?" He concluded that both are correct because they view the event from different frames of reference.

A second well-known example of a thought experiment is Plato's "Allegory of the Cave," in which he explores the nature of human perception, the soul, and contemplation of the divine. He imagined prisoners who had been chained in a cave from childhood so that all they could see were the shadows of people and objects cast upon the cave wall in front of them. He also suggested that the prisoners would think that the echoes of voices bouncing off the back of the cave were the voices of the shadow people. By exploring this imagined situation, Plato concluded that while we may form perceptions through our experience of objects, we would be incorrect if we thought those perceptions were the same as the objects themselves.

In the thought experiment to discover a name for your genius, you will need to imagine that eight conditions are true. These eight conditions are purposefully restrictive in order to give definition to the idea of genius and to provide a framework for your thought experiment. They are the what-ifs of your experiment. Imagine that they are true, much as Plato imagined people chained in a cave and Einstein imagined people on a moving train. Once you accept the conditions, you will be prepared to continue the thought experiment to name your genius. These are the eight conditions:

1. You do have a genius. I can offer no scientific proof that you have a genius. I have only my experience and the experiences of the many others who have found their geniuses. You will either prove or fail to prove to yourself that you have a genius. The only way to do that is to become involved in this thought experiment. In other words, suspend any disbelief, keep reading, and do the exercises in this book.

2. You have only one genius. At some point in the thought experiment, you may come to believe that you have two or more geniuses. A condition of the experiment is that you have only one. This condition is important as it forces you to think more deeply about yourself. When people conclude that they have more than one genius, it is because they have not yet found the true genius. For example, Lyall thought he had two names for his genius. One was Walking the Landscape, and the other was Looking for Truth. Walking the Landscape described his tendency to seek new ideas, thoughts, and experiences. When he realized that his metaphorical walking was in search of truth or new ideas and that the word *walking* seemed too passive a description of what he did, he combined the two names into Surveying the Landscape.

3. Your genius has been with you for your entire life. Your genius is not a transient or a temporary thing. It has always been with you. It is natural to your being. When you recognize your genius, you will see that you engaged it even as a small child. Joyce, who calls her genius Digging Deeper, said, "My genius gets up in the morning before I do." Tia, whose genius is Taking Care, said, "I know that my genius has been with me always. I believe it is undeniably and unavoidably the energy of my soul."

4. Your genius is natural and spontaneous and a source of success. Your genius is often engaged in your activities without your noticing it, or it comes so naturally to you that it seems unremarkable or obvious. Yet it creates joy and success for you when used in the right situations.

5. Your genius is a positive force. If you arrive at a name for your genius that feels negative to you, it does not describe your genius. Your genius is a positive force, an expression of what is good and right about you. At times, your genius may be engaged inappropriately, or for damaging ends, but your genius itself is positive. While there is no doubt that evil exists in the world, the evil is not a product of genius. The so-called evil genius, a brilliant but destructive force, is a result of turning that positive force to destructive ends.

6. Your genius is not what you wish it would be; it is what it is. Be certain that the name you choose truly describes your genius and not what you think it should be or what you think might sound good to others. For example, in workshops sponsored by organizations, people frequently come up with names like Playing on a Team and Taking Risks. These names often arise when the organization is trying to encourage team play or risk taking. You must look beneath these terms to find your genius. In this case, underneath Playing on a Team might be something like Making Connections or Building Energy, names that better describe a unique contribution.

7. Your name for your genius should contain one gerund and one noun. A gerund is a verb that ends with the suffix *ing*. Use a gerund in the name for your genius in order to indicate that the action expressed by the word is always in progress. Your genius is not an event, goal, or outcome but a process. It is not static but ongoing. You can see how a gerund functions in the examples above: Surveying the Landscape, Digging Deeper, Taking Care.

8. Your name for your genius will be unique. The list below contains names that people have chosen for their geniuses. As you read the list, avoid the temptation to say, "That name fits me too." Go through the process of finding your own name for your genius. The process is one of discovery rather than selection. Among the many hundreds of names that I have heard used to describe geniuses, I cannot recall hearing the same name twice. Your genius is your unique gift, and I encourage you to discover the unique name for it. If one of the names below does resonate with you, treat that as a clue to your genius rather than the final word. Each of the names below is described in more detail in this book.

Engaging the Heart

Digging Deeper

Pursuing Understanding

Taking Care

Straightening Up

Finding the Positive

Making It Work

Feeling Deeply

Searching for Clues

Generating Warmth

Charting the Course

Building Platforms

Exploring Pathways

Finding Jewels

THE BASIC PROCESS

There are three basic components to the process of recognizing your genius. The first component is **noticing** certain aspects of your experience. Clues about your genius will be found in two kinds of experiences, current and past. As you read and do the exercises, notice your experiences with soft eyes that are observant and accepting rather than hard eyes that are critical and judgmental. Noticing is an information-gathering process.

The second component is **associating** the information you notice. When you notice something that seems like it might be a clue to your genius, ask, "What else do I do that seems similar?" Associate freely, trusting your intuition, and without censoring yourself.

The third component of the process is **looking beneath** the surface information that you gather about yourself. Your genius is an undercurrent sweeping along below the surface of your activities. In order to find the undercurrent, approach the process of recognizing your genius in a spirit of curiosity about yourself. Do not analyze yourself or condemn your motives. Just be curious about what you do naturally and spontaneously. Remember that the purpose of the exercises and suggestions is to collect information, associate it, and look beneath it, not to analyze or judge it.

AHA!

Read the **introduction in the exercises section** (pages 113–114) and use **Exercise 1** (page 118) to find words for your genius.

The moment of recognizing your genius will be an Aha! experience—a sudden and powerful flash of insight about yourself.

An event reported by physicist Werner Heisenberg is a good example of an Aha! experience. In 1926, Heisenberg and fellow physicist Niels Bohr spent many long nights in Copenhagen, Denmark, arguing and puzzling over newly born theories of quantum mechanics. In February 1927, Bohr decided to get away from it all to go skiing in Norway. Heisenberg was glad to be left behind, where, as he wrote, "I could think about these hopelessly complicated problems undisturbed."[4]

This is much the same as puzzling for hours, days, or months over your genius and then taking some time away from the process in order to let it percolate.

In his writing about this period of solitude, Heisenberg describes the obstacles before him as insurmountable. He wonders if he and Bohr have been asking the wrong questions and tries to make connections between seemingly mutually exclusive facts. Heisenberg wrote:

> I was immediately convinced that the key to the gate that had been closed for so long must be sought right here. I decided to go on a nocturnal walk through Faelle Park and to think further about the matter.[5]

While he was on this walk, Heisenberg formulated what is now known as the uncertainty principle of quantum mechanics. It was a breakthrough that changed the world of physics. Later, he wrote that his theory "established the much needed bridge."[6]

Heisenberg's famous walk in the park demonstrates what happens when someone has an Aha! experience. He and his associates had been puzzling over their problem for months—studying it, reading about it, and talking with one another. Then Heisenberg let go, and the answer appeared. Such letting go, walking away from a problem, is often necessary to the creative leap that produces the Aha! experience.

Experts in creativity explain this phenomenon as a product of the unconscious breaking through to the conscious. While you are consciously using the exercises provided here to help you find a name for your genius, your subconscious will be working at the same task. Letting go of your efforts, stopping the active conscious process of collecting information about your genius, may allow the subconscious to break through and reveal the work that it has been doing to recognize your genius.

Alberto arrived at a name for his genius while jogging. Some people find the names in dreams. One man was fishing for trout.

As you work your way through the exercises in this book, you will fill your conscious mind with information. Then let it go for a while. The Aha! is your subconscious breaking through the chatter of your conscious mind. You cannot make this happen. All you can do is divert yourself with some relatively mindless activity like a walk, a jog, a nap, or a lazy hour or two alongside a trout stream.

When you have discovered the right name for your genius, you will know it. I have watched many people recognize their geniuses. Almost always, when they have it right, they know it, and I can see that they know it. A look of recognition and pleasure spreads across their faces. Watch for that feeling. When you experience it, you will know that you have gotten it right.

Notice Yourself

The real voyage of discovery consists not in seeking new landscapes but in having new eyes.

—MARCEL PROUST

IT WAS HALF PAST SEVEN in the morning, and the June air was already steamy in the small nature preserve. I sat on a wooden bench, sipping coffee, seeking whatever lessons might be drawn from the river that flowed about ten feet in front of me. In the previous few days, the river had cleared itself of the muddiness it carries after heavy spring and early summer rains. Its new emerald-hued clarity reflected the canopy of broad oak trees that surrounded and shaded me.

The crack of a fallen twig called my attention to a man walking the narrow dirt trail that led to the bench. He was wearing heavy, scuffed shoes, a well-worn black-and-yellow plaid work shirt, and faded khaki pants. He had not shaved recently; gray stubble covered his jaw. I guessed that he was in his sixties. He smiled as if to assure me that he was an OK fellow.

"River's getting back to normal," he said, stopping behind the bench, peering over my shoulder and through the trees at the slow-moving water.

I was not sure that I wanted conversation just then, so I murmured a reluctant "Yes."

"A few weeks ago," he said, "it was so high that it covered this bench you're sitting on."

He sat beside me, and I knew that if I didn't want conversation, I would have to leave. I decided to stay.

He extended his hand. "My name is Clyde. Haven't seen you here before."

I introduced myself. "So you come here a lot?" I asked.

He said, "Yes. I hang out here since I got laid off a few months ago. I needed something to do so I volunteered to take care of the park. I open the gates in the morning, hang out most of the day, go home for dinner, then come back until it's time to close the gate at sundown. It keeps me busy, and I like it here."

During the few times that I had visited the preserve, I had not noticed Clyde. I felt sure, however, that he had noticed me and that he was curious about this newcomer to his domain. I asked questions, he answered, and in the course of about ten minutes, I learned that he had been a maintenance man in a warehouse, that he lived with and cared for an elderly sister, and that he owned two rental properties.

As he told these stories, I found myself listening between the lines for clues to his genius. It is an amusing game, like assembling a jigsaw puzzle. First, you must examine the pieces one by one—he was a maintenance man, he cares for his sister, he owns several properties. Then you must find how pieces fit together. Maintenance work is about taking care of something, or fixing something. He spent his time caring for the park, taking care of his elderly sister, whom he described as "not right," and doing most of the repair work on his rental properties. Finally, you must begin to see how the whole picture comes together. Clyde was taking care, fixing, maintaining, making things right, and so forth. It occurred to me that if I were to have trouble with my car as I left the park, Clyde would show up in the parking lot to help out. The problem with this analogy is that, unlike a jigsaw puzzle, your genius does not come in a box with a picture of itself on the cover, so your task is more challenging.

While I could not say what Clyde would name his genius, I was certain that there were many clues within the stories he had told about himself. I began to think that Clyde's genius had something to do with taking care, or perhaps it was about fixing.

FIELDS OF INFORMATION

Recognizing your genius is mostly a matter of gathering pertinent information about yourself and then working with the information in a way that yields a name for your genius. There are many rather simple and direct ways of gathering pertinent information. One of them is explained below; others are covered in Chapter 5 and in the exercises section. Each of these ways of gathering information describes a fertile field and suggestions about how to explore it. For example, in the course of my conversation with Clyde, he offered information from several fields of his experience: what he enjoys, what he gives to the park and to those who visit it, and times in his life when he felt successful.

The first field of information in which to search for your genius is **noticing what you do when you are not noticing what you do.** Yes, it sounds paradoxical, but your genius comes spontaneously and easily. It is so natural to you that you probably do not notice it. This is an important field of information because it requires attending to information that you usually ignore. You ignore this information when you do not notice behavior that comes naturally to you. Attending to such information enables you to see yourself in a new and different way.

For example, many people in management roles pay attention to only one kind of information, intellectual information expressed in thoughts, ideas, and numbers. They often ignore emotional information, even when their own emotions are in play. Yet the feelings people have about their work and what happens in their workplace have an enormous impact on their performance. Paying attention to emotional information would induce managers to behave very differently because they would see things they do not normally see.

The following lines are a powerful reminder about the importance of noticing what you do not usually notice:

> If I continue to take in data as I have always taken in data,
> Then I will continue to think as I have always thought.
> If I continue to think as I have always thought,
> Then I will continue to believe as I have always believed.
> If I continue to believe as I have always believed,
> Then I will continue to act as I have always acted.
> If I continue to act as I have always acted,
> Then I will continue to get what I have always gotten.[1]

These lines suggest that using information unlike the kind you normally use will open the door to change in your life and work. The stories told in this book, about people who have gained knowledge of their genius, attest to the profound difference such knowledge can make.

Recognizing your genius provides a way of seeing yourself and your work in a fresh way, creating a new belief. Because of that new belief, you may act differently. Because of this different action, you may get something other than what you have always gotten. In order to set this chain of causality in motion, you will have to attend to another kind of information.

Once you have begun gathering information, you also have to work with it until you recognize your genius and a name emerges. This process, unlike that of gathering the information, is no simple matter. It is an organic, creative challenge to produce an Aha! experience. Your process will be as unique to you as is your genius. That explains why I cannot say what Clyde's genius is; he would have to engage in his unique process and arrive at a name that holds meaning for him. In short, there is no magic formula for finding the right name for your genius.

Given, then, the absence of a magic formula, I can direct you to three approaches, or ways of working with the information, that might help you gain the Aha! you are seeking.

- Imagine that the information you have collected about yourself lies on the outer layers of an onion and that your genius lies at the center.

- Find the common denominator in all of the information.

- Discover the shared thread of intent that lies beneath all of the information.

Peeling the Onion

The process of recognizing your genius is much like peeling an onion (see the diagram on page 32). Imagine an onion in which the outer layers represent your skills, talents, behavior, accomplishments, interests, and creations. You have developed the talents and skills you most enjoy because they allow expression of your genius. They are the means by which your genius comes alive. When you peel all the outer layers away, you will recognize your genius at the center.

For example, I call my genius Creating Clarity. I have developed skills in communication, writing, photography, and teaching because they allow me to create clarity. Genius itself lies beneath those skills and talents, nearer to the center of the onion.

I recognized my genius in the mid-1980s. It took me several months to arrive at a satisfactory name. Creating clarity is about understanding the world. It is about discovering ways of grasping complex ideas and phenomena. For example, in my work as a consultant to organizations and to individuals concerned with their own growth, I develop conceptual models that explain such things as customer service, career management, organizational purpose, self-responsibility, leadership, teamwork, and empowerment. I develop these models so that I can understand the phenomena that are important to my clients. I also find that my

Skills

Behavior

Interests

GENIUS

Talents

Creations

Accomplishments

models are useful to others in planning processes and programs that deal with those issues. My skill at building conceptual models is near the skin of the onion; it is not my genius, which lies deeper.

I also love teaching because it helps me come to new awareness—greater clarity—about whatever subject I am teaching. I have taught mathematics, psychology, career management, organizational change, management theory, team development, and customer service. I most enjoy teaching about something when I feel a need for greater clarity about it. Teaching, like creating conceptual models, is also a skill, nearer the surface of the onion.

My genius is also at work in my hobbies. I am an amateur carpenter. I built a deck on my house and finished a hot tub room with tongue-and-groove cedar. I am clear about how to do those projects but have no wish to repeat the experiences, even though they were pleasurable.

I am also an amateur photographer who tries to create clear images that provoke questions. One of my favorite photographs shows two joggers, a man and a woman, resting on the steps of a church in Key West, Florida. Dressed in a black T-shirt and shorts, the dark-haired man sits leaning forward, elbows on his knees, chin resting in his hands, covered by the shadows of a tree. The woman, in contrast, is in full sunlight. Her jogging suit is white, her hair blond. She leans back, legs stretched out in front of her. The man's eyes are downcast, but the woman looks at him through the bars of the wrought iron railing that separates them. In short, the two people in this photograph are contrasts of light and shadow, open and closed. The railing between them suggests a barrier.

When others look at this image, they react in much the same way I did when I first saw it: "What is going on here?" Soon the picture becomes clear, although different people come to different conclusions about what is happening in the scene. Some conclude that the two people are angry at each other. Others believe he is ignoring her, while she is trying to attract his attention. Others merely see two people resting. This photograph represents the essence of my genius: looking at something familiar but not well understood and coming to some clarity about it. Many of my best photographs are like that.

Use **Exercise 2** to examine your skills, talents, behavior, accomplishments, interests, and creations for clues to your genius (see page 120).

Like teaching, carpentry and photography are near the surface of the onion. They are skills I have developed in part because they give expression to my genius.

To me, there is one significant similarity in developing a theoretical model to explain customer service, teaching a variety of subjects, writing about things I don't quite understand, building a deck mostly to figure out how to build a deck, and taking photographs that force the viewer to ask and answer the question "What is going on here?" All of those enterprises are about the same thing: creating clarity.

When you recognize your genius, you will see that it is active in all of the important domains of your life: relationships, work, hobbies, spiritual practices, and family life. You will also have a potent tool that helps in making important choices and decisions within those domains.

The activities I engage in and described above are the outer layer of the onion that I had to peel in order to find my genius underneath. When you have peeled away all the outer layers to find the core—your genius—you will experience the Aha! Like the onion, the Aha! might bring tears to your eyes, the kind of tears you experience when greeting an old and treasured friend whom you have not seen for a long time.

Finding the Common Denominator

Another way to approach the information that you gather is to look within it to seek a common denominator. In mathematics, a common denominator is the number by which every number in a series can be divided. Ask yourself what words might describe your genius and then try to discover what they have in common—what "goes into" all of them. As an illustration of the notion, find the lowest common denominator in each of these three lines of numbers:

4, 6, 12, 24, 100

9, 15, 21, 30

15, 25, 65, 90

The lowest common denominators are 2 for the first line, 3 for the second, and 5 for the third.

It is not so simple to find the common denominator within the information you gather about your genius, because that common denominator is not as apparent. It is not your ordinary common denominator. As an example, find the common denominator among these numbers:

2, 10, 13, 29, 300

The common denominator for that line of numbers is the letter *t*, because the words for those numbers begin with a *t*: two, ten, thirteen, twenty-nine, and three hundred. This common denominator lies beneath the surface of the numbers themselves. It is not immediately apparent, just as your genius may not be immediately apparent in your activities. You will have to dig for it and look underneath the surface information.

Dave's story is an example of noticing what you do when you are not noticing what you do. It also illustrates the approach of finding the common denominator for all the information you notice. Dave is a chemical engineer who had been in a managerial job at a chemical company for two years. He was bored with his job and concerned that his boredom was beginning to influence his performance. He arrived at a career development workshop eager to figure out what he might do about his boredom and its potential consequences. He was also asking himself if taking on managerial responsibilities had been a mistake.

This workshop was focused on recognizing each person's genius, and for the first day and a half, Dave sought his genius with much enthusiasm but little success. After the lunch break on the second day of the workshop, he returned to our meeting room before anyone else. A flip chart at the front of the room held a large pad of paper. The pad had been rolled up before being placed on its stand and did not lie flat. A large potted plant stood in a corner. It had been knocked awry and leaned crookedly.

Dave walked into the room, went to the flip chart and flattened it with his hand, went to the plant and straightened it, arranged the chairs, and then sat down. The group reconvened and began talking about what they had been noticing about themselves.

Dave said, "I didn't notice myself doing it while I was doing it, but I notice it now. When I came into the room, I fixed the flip chart, straightened the plant, and put the chairs back in place. It just seemed like the natural thing to do—to tidy up the room. I didn't think about it. I just did it."

This type of behavior is usually a clue to your genius; it is spontaneous, unplanned, and carried out with little or no awareness. It is what you do when you are not noticing what you do.

After Dave noticed what he had done, he began to make associations between this behavior and other aspects of his life. He told the group about his home workshop, where he got as much enjoyment out of organizing his tools and supplies as anything else he did there. He also talked about his first days at his current job, when the group he managed was in disarray. Priorities were unclear. A lot of the work being done was unnecessary. Conflict was rampant within the group and between the group and other groups in the company. Customers were confused and unhappy. He talked about how he had cleaned up the mess he had found there and commented that things were now running smoothly.

Dave saw that there was a common denominator for his behavior when he had entered the room, in his home workshop, and on his first days at his current job.

He said, "The common denominator in all of those situations is that I am straightening up." Then Dave recognized the genius that had eluded him. He named it Straightening Up.

Dave had also answered the second of the four key questions. He knew immediately after recognizing his genius that it had not been at work because there was nothing more for him to straighten up. Dave needs messes.

Recognizing his genius was an important milestone in Dave's career. He resolved to seek jobs and tasks that will allow him to bring his genius into play. Assuming managerial responsibility is not a mistake for Dave as long the situations he manages give him opportunities to straighten up.

Discovering the Shared Thread of Intent

The third approach to the information that you gather is to examine the entire collection of information for a shared thread of intent. This shared thread of intent is usually unconscious. For example, unless I am fully aware of my genius, I believe the intent of counseling or consulting is to help others, and I believe the intent of doing research is to gain new knowledge. Those are, however, merely my conscious intentions. The underlying intent, which is creating clarity, lurks underneath my conscious intent.

The story of how June recognized her genius is another illustration of noticing what you are doing when you are not noticing what you are doing and also of finding a shared thread of intent in what you noticed.

During a workshop similar to the one Dave attended, June noticed that she took notes in a much more comprehensive and disciplined way than anyone else. She also noticed that she was the one who suggested that the group create a list of names and phone numbers so that people could stay in touch after the workshop. She felt compelled to do that for the group, even though nobody had asked for a phone list.

This behavior felt familiar to June, and she immediately began to associate it with other activities that she does routinely. You will know that you are on the right track when associations between other activities and what you notice come to you quickly and easily. June talked about two hobbies, sewing and gardening. She was not an avid seamstress, but she did enjoy buying patterns and had a drawer full of them. Although she felt that she would never use some of the patterns, she was comforted by their presence in her home. They were available whenever she felt the urge to sew. As a gardener, she enjoyed planning, preparing, and planting much more than tending the garden. She felt compelled to engage in these activities and very much enjoyed them.

June said that her intent in each activity had something to do with creating a base from which to launch other activities. The phone list was a database. The patterns were a base for sewing. Planning, preparing, and planting a garden created a base for growing flowers and vegetables.

She also associated what she had noticed with a job change she was contemplating. She worked for a large corporation that was undergoing the upheaval familiar to many of today's companies. Although trained as a systems analyst, she had accepted a temporary assignment on a team the company had formed to help it through a complex change process. The team led training programs and helped other teams become more effective. June loved this work.

Finally, after much discussion and rumination, June discovered the shared thread of intent in all of the activities she had spoken about. Her notes, the phone list, the patterns, and the garden preparations are all platforms. She took copious notes because she wanted to use them as a platform to continue learning after the workshop. The phone list was a platform upon which to create a support network of people engaged in recognizing their genius. Her drawer full of patterns was a platform she could utilize whenever she felt the urge to sew. As a gardener, she got the most pleasure out of preparing the platform for her garden. And June's new work was exciting because she saw herself as helping to create a platform that would aid her company in dealing with change and attaining future prosperity. She created many platforms for herself and so wanted to provide others in the company with a platform as well.

June arrived at the name Building Platforms to describe her genius. When she recognized her genius, it became immediately apparent to her why she enjoyed her new role in the company. She had answered the second of the four key questions: her genius was very much at work in her job.

Although June recognized her genius by seeking the shared intent among several activities, she might also have looked for a common denominator. Before she arrived at the name Building Platforms, she talked of creating a phone list, buying patterns, and planning a garden. The words *creating*, *buying*, and *planning* didn't feel quite right to her as terms to describe her genius. There was no felt sense of rightness about them. The same was true for the terms *phone list*, *patterns*, and *garden*. The right name for her genius is the common denominator for the two sets of words: *creating, buying,* and *planning* are about "building," and *phone list, patterns,* and *garden* are about "platforms."

After recognizing her genius and answering the question "What is your purpose?" June made an important career choice. She committed to a new career path as an organizational change agent. This path seemed right to her not only because it engaged her genius but also because she saw that her analytical training, her decision to work for a large corporation, and the invitation to be part of the company's change team had all prepared her to pursue a new purpose—building platforms upon which healthy and productive human organizations could be built.

Use **Exercise 3** to begin noticing what you do when you are not noticing what you do (see page 122).

FOUR WARNINGS!

The process of finding a name for your genius may go astray in four ways.

First, a particular genius sometimes works in a way that makes it difficult to name the genius. For example, Marcel had a difficult time settling on a name for his genius. As soon as he believed he had the right name, he immediately began considering alternatives. When he noticed himself doing that, the correct name became obvious to him. His genius is indeed Considering Alternatives. Myra, whose genius is Getting to the Bottom, had a similar difficulty. Each time she settled on a name, she would seek one underneath it. She too noticed what she was doing and acknowledged that her genius is Getting to the Bottom.

Second, the process goes astray if you approach your genius at a level that is too abstract or too general to express your uniqueness, arriving at names such as Helping Others or Doing Good. You almost always try to employ your genius with the intent of helping others or doing good, so such names do not sufficiently differentiate your genius from others. They don't provide you with a real sense of your uniqueness. The question is, What is your special way of helping others or doing good? Although abstract or general names do not describe a genius, your desire to choose them as names is a valuable clue. For example, Ann, a nurse, first thought her genius was Helping Others. When challenged to peel the onion further, she realized that her true genius was Feeling Deeply. Because she feels things deeply, she empathizes easily with others and wants to help them. As a rule, avoid using the words *others* and *people* when finding a name for your genius.

Third, the process may go astray if you feel disheartened when a name for your genius does not appear quickly and easily. Dave and June were each able to recognize their geniuses within the time frame of a workshop, but for most people, the process takes much longer. For example, it took me several months.

And fourth, you can go astray by avoiding strong words. Some people are reluctant to speak of themselves in bold terms. For example, at a conference some years ago a woman described herself to me as a "fiber artist." Later, when we were in a group together, she introduced herself by saying, "I make quilts." When I asked her about the discrepancy, she said, "I do think of myself as a fiber artist, but it sounds too lofty." People often take a similar approach by choosing a name such as Bringing Energy when Lighting the Fire would be more descriptive. Find the words that are truly descriptive and put aside any tendency to minimize your own natural power. Keep in mind these words from Marianne Williamson: "Our deepest fear is not that we are inadequate. Our deepest fear is that we are powerful beyond measure."[2]

TRY IT ON

If you have an idea about what your genius might be, write its name in the name tag. Do not worry about being "right." Simply record your best guess at the moment. Be sure to express your genius as a process, using one word that ends with *ing* and one noun.

You may believe that you have the right name for your genius now. If you do, try saying aloud, "My genius is _____ _____." See how it feels. Does it feel right, or does some nagging doubt lurk within you? Whatever happens, trust it. Most people go through many names before finding one that feels just right. Do not worry about that. Accept the name you have for your genius now, if you have one, and continue. If the name you have is right, it will still feel right as you go on. If it is not, you will get closer to the right name as you continue.

The next chapter describes the many facets of genius and its myriad descriptions in different spiritual and cultural traditions. The intent is to deepen your understanding of the concept of genius, not necessarily to help you recognize yours. In Chapter 5, we return to describing methods that will help you recognize your genius.

Find the Face
of Genius

How can I be useful, of what service can I be?
There is something inside me, what can it be?

—VINCENT VAN GOGH

GENIUS IS AN ANCIENT CONCEPT that is enjoying a renaissance. It has lived for a long time in the shadows of Western culture. Rediscovered, the image of genius is nonetheless faded and blurred, like an old photograph of a forgotten relative. We look at the image and ask, "Who is that? How are we related?" Genius belongs to the realm of mystery, together with spirit and soul, and so exactly who or what it is, and how it is related to us, will probably never be perfectly clear.

There are many reasons for our indistinct image of genius. Even within spiritual and cultural traditions that acknowledged genius in the past, or that now appreciate it, the terms referring to it carry different shades of meaning among various factions, sects, religions, and tribes. Different people have different names for it, and those names change over time. For example, it was called *daimon* in classical Greece. *Daimon* became the *demon* of contemporary culture, and it is said that we humans gain protection from demons through guardian angels. Guardian angels bear some resemblance to the original *daimons*, which were also protective spirits. The migration of meaning from *daimon* to *demon* led to the term's current malevolent connotations; originally, the word *daimon* did not connote evil.

Also, various traditions carve up the sacred realm in different ways, assigning spiritual experiences and beliefs to this or that concept according to their own cosmologies. For example, the boundary between genius and soul is drawn differently by different peoples. The ancient Greeks and Romans saw genius as an intermediary between physical reality and a pantheon of gods, Christians view it as a connection to the one true God of the Bible, and it is seen as a liaison with ancestors in some African traditions. Wherever the cosmology enfolding a particular image of genius is very different from our own, the image appears more foreign to us.

The renaissance of genius has been encouraged by Wayne Dyer in *The Power of Intention*, James Hillman in *The Soul's Code*, Deepak Chopra in *Seven Spiritual Laws of Success*, Gary Zukav in *Seat of the Soul*, Malidoma Somé in *The Healing Wisdom of Africa*, and Robert Bly in *The Sibling Society*.

Hillman approached the challenge of understanding genius by referring to the entire historical body of beliefs about genius as "acorn theory," which he described as "each person bears a uniqueness that asks to be lived and that is already present before it is lived."[1] Hillman's idea is useful because it recognizes that "you and I and every single person is born with a defining image" and acknowledges the pervasiveness of genius across traditions.[2] It also validates the idea that something beyond our rational understanding, and outside the experience and skills catalogued in our résumés, functions as the seed of our individual greatness. I refer to that something as your *genius*. I have chosen that term because it is familiar, and because the Roman concept to which it refers encompasses most of the characteristics of genius that are important to decisions about your work and career.

Even though the image of genius is blurred, it has been portrayed well enough that you can construct a meaningful and valuable picture of it. In this chapter, we take a break from trying to recognize your unique genius in order to deepen understanding of the concept itself. For all of the reasons above, I will attempt not to present a clear definition so much as to put forward a variety of images of genius. Mystery is located closer to intuition and belief than to rational thought, so mystery is better appreciated through imagery than definition.

In this chapter, I describe how my image of genius emerged over the twenty years I have been studying it. I do not intend to persuade you that any particular image or characteristic of genius is correct or better than any other. Rather, I want to describe the essential characteristics of genius. By doing so, I hope to enable you to construct an image of genius that seems true to you, or to find the concept as it exists in your own spiritual or cultural tradition.

A VARIETY OF IMAGES

In order to begin finding an image of genius that seems true to you, imagine that representative artists from various spiritual and cultural traditions have each created a depiction of genius. Their respective images would make sense to others who share the tradition because it would reflect that tradition's beliefs. For example, William Blake, rooted in Christianity, painted genius as a hovering winged angel offering a cornucopia of gifts to a poet strumming a lyre, a decidedly Christian image. In contrast, an Egyptian artist living at the time of the pharaohs might depict genius—he or she would call it *ba*—as a birdlike figure with a human head. A Native American artist might show genius in the form of a personal totem animal. Not surprisingly, genius takes on aspects of the tradition within which it is described.

As another example of the difficulty of finding a clear image of genius, I must note that the Egyptian artist might have painted, instead of the bird-man *ba*, an image of an associated spirit, *ka*. The line between the concepts of *ba* and *ka* is unclear to us, and each might be seen as having properties that other traditions would associate with genius. If the Egyptian artist had chosen to depict *ka*, he or she would have shown a smaller version of a person standing behind the full image of the person. *Ka* was viewed as a spiritual double.

While each of the representative artists would depict genius differently, if we were to examine the beliefs that gave form to their images, we would see among them common characteristics—striking similarities—that mark the image as a picture of genius. We will focus on the following common themes:

- Genius is a gift from the divine.

- Genius acts as an intermediary between the divine and the everyday.

- The purpose of genius is to serve others.

- Each person's genius is unique.

- Genius comes naturally.

- Genius is a source of protection and guidance.

- It is dangerous to abandon or ignore your genius.

Each of the belief systems that inform the images portrayed by our supposed artists might lack one or more of these characteristics. The differences in various traditions are interesting to explore if you wish to travel the road of comparative spiritual and cultural studies, but they are secondary to the purpose of recognizing your own genius. There is consensus about genius among spiritual and cultural traditions, if not full agreement on every point.

THE BEGINNING

I was introduced to the concept that I now call "genius" by my friend and colleague Calvin Germain, who called it "Core Process."

Calvin described Core Process as the spontaneous and unique sequence of events that happens within you when you encounter information from the external world and then react to it.

To understand the idea of Core Process, imagine yourself as a box. Information comes into the box at one end, something happens to the information inside the box, and something comes out of the box at the other end. The activity that takes place inside the box is the Core Process. For me, the Core Process involves scanning the world for things I want to understand and then proceeding to understanding them. My shorthand way of saying that—my name for my genius—is Creating Clarity.

Although I now prefer to call it "genius," I still find the notion of Core Process useful. It evokes the idea that genius resides at my core, at the very center of who I am. It also recognizes genius as an ongoing process rather than a result.

The idea of Core Process served me well during the early phases of learning about genius, but the term seemed lacking in some way that I could not comprehend. During a workshop on Core Process, a woman who had been reared in the Hindu tradition told me that the concept sounded very much like *dharma,* which she described as the essential quality of a person. I later discovered that the term *dharma* has many different meanings, but the woman's comment opened the door leading to the spiritual dimension of genius and hinted at what was lacking in my understanding of Core Process.

Connecting Core Process to *dharma* started me on a search that unearthed many manifestations of genius, each of them differing from the others in some attributes but together showing the way to the seven characteristics listed above. Among these multiple manifestations are the *daimon* of Plato's Greece, *neshama* in Hebrew cosmology, *ka* and *ba* in the Egypt of the pharaohs, *Teh* in Taoism, *pneuma* from the Hellenistic era, the *ase* of the Yoruba, Christianity's guardian angels, Native American totems, *siura* from the Dagara tribe of West Africa, the *nagual* in Mesoamerica, and many others.

THE DIVINE GIFT

We begin fleshing out the seven characteristics of genius with an introduction to Plato's *daimon*. In the tenth book of *The Republic*, Plato describes the passage of souls into mortal existence. They are brought in a group before Lachesis, one of the three Fates. She holds in her lap a quantity of lots and another quantity of patterns of life. Each soul chooses a lot and then, in the order of the lots, souls select from among the patterns of life. After picking its pattern of life, the soul chooses its *daimon*. Plato writes, "And when all the souls had made their choice, they went before Lachesis in the order of their lots, and she allotted to each its chosen Guardian Spirit, to guide it through life and fulfill its choice."[3] Plato's *daimon* —translated above as "Guardian Spirit"—then leads the soul through the remainder of the process that gives it a mortal reality. Thus, the genius is chosen by the soul as guide and protector for the life that it is about to begin.

The notion of genius as a divine gift echoes everywhere genius is present. Saint Jerome writes, "How great the dignity of the soul, since each one has from his birth an angel commissioned to guard it."[4] *Ka* represented the receiving of capabilities from the gods. Hillman summarized the idea of genius as a gift, using the term *character* as a synonym for *genius*: "You are born with a character; it is given; a gift, as the old stories say, from the guardians upon your birth."[5]

Beliefs about the source of the divine gift differ. Unlike the Greeks of the classical period, who saw it as a gift from the gods, the Dagara view it as emanating from ancestors. The time and means of its appearance also vary. Native American *totems,* for example, are given in dreams, initiation rituals, and periods of solitude rather than before birth.

It is interesting to note another aspect of Plato's tale as you attempt to recognize your genius. Near the end of the soul's passage into mortal existence, it is brought to the River of Forgetting and told to drink the water. Upon doing so, the soul forgets everything. It forgets former existences, forgets what has happened in the world between lives, forgets its choice of life pattern, and forgets its genius.

This forgetting seems important; it is mirrored in other lore as well. In Buddhist legend, Old Lady Meng doles out the Broth of Oblivion to souls returning to earth. And in Jewish tradition, "God granted Adam and Eve an all-important blessing as they were about to leave the Garden of Eden: I give you, He said, 'the gift of forgetfulness.'"[6]

Neither Plato, Buddhist legend, nor Jewish tradition tells us the purpose of this forgetting. Perhaps there is something essential about the effort to remember what has been forgotten, something necessary about the often challenging process of recognizing your genius.

THE INTERMEDIARY

Plato's *daimon* is not of the soul; it is chosen by the soul. It is not of the divine; it is given by the divine. It is also not of the body; it accompanies the body. It occupies an intermediate existence. This idea found expression in Hellenistic cosmology as *pneuma*, which was believed to act as a vehicle or vessel that carries the soul and links it to the body. *Ka* had the power to travel between the spiritual and human worlds. In both the Old and the New Testament, angels are intermediaries between God and man.

The view that genius represents the presence of the divine in a person is akin to the idea that genius is distinct from the divine, the soul, and the body. In Hebrew, *neshama* is the presence of God in you. The Egyptian *ka* is your expression of life's vital energy, your unique way of participating in what the Chinese would call *ch'i*, a Hindu, *prana*, and a Taoist, *Tao*.

Your genius, then, is your link to the divine.

Seen from this perspective, Francine's story, which explains how her genius seemed unwelcome in the company for which she worked (see Chapter 1), takes on a profound meaning: it was not merely her ability and passion to engage the heart that was rejected but her unique expression of the presence of God in her. Viewed in this way, her anger, hurt, and frustration become thoroughly understandable.

SERVICE TO OTHERS

I refer to "your genius" throughout this book, but it is merely a linguistic convenience. There is a sense of genius in which it is not yours at all but belongs to everyone else. This sense is conveyed by the Bible in Corinthians, "To each one is given the manifestation of the Spirit for the common good," and in Peter, "As each one has received a special gift, employ it in serving one another as good stewards of the manifold grace of God."[7] And we commonly refer to someone who performs a good deed as an "angel."

The idea of your genius as a spirit given to you for the common good is also present in Jewish thought: "We have an obligation to find that special treasure within ourselves and share it with others."[8]

In the *Tao Te Ching*, Lao Tzu discusses *Teh*, which is often translated as "Mystic Virtue"; it refers to the power of each person to be uniquely whoever he or she is and to participate in the *Tao*, the source of existence that nourishes and sustains everything. Lao Tzu writes, "Possessing *Teh* is to act out of love without ulterior motive."[9]

One of the more eloquent expressions of genius in service to others comes from the Dagara of West Africa. Malidoma Somé writes that when a Dagara woman becomes pregnant, people in her village ask, "Why is this person being sent to us at this time? What gifts will this person have that our community needs?" Rituals are performed in which the fetus's life force is asked what the child will bring to the community.[10]

There are also hints that genius thrives in a community in which it is recognized and celebrated. Dagara communities take responsibility for awakening and nurturing the gift, recognizing that the community's vitality flows from that of its members. Somé writes, "The newborn must be assisted in giving birth to the genius that he is born with. Failure to do so kills that genius along with the person carrying it."[11]

Greeks and Romans honored a genius on its birthday, sometimes offering sacrifices to that spirit.

And so it seems that your genius is not yours after all, and that you have, perhaps, not just the option of recognizing your special treasure, but an obligation to discover it and direct it to the common good. Your genius is your unique way of making a beneficial difference in the world.

UNIQUENESS

Your genius is a gift from the divine that acts as an intermediary between the divine, the soul, and the body and is the source of your positive contribution to the world. It is also unique to you.

In *The Seven Spiritual Laws of Success*, Deepak Chopra describes his seventh law as the Law of Dharma. Chopra writes,

> You have a talent that is unique in its expression, so unique that there is no one else alive on this planet that has that talent, or that expression of that talent. This means that there is one thing you can do, and one way of doing it, that is better than any one else on this entire planet.[12]

Similarly, among the Yoruba, the term *ase* is used to describe, in the words of professor of religion John Pemberton III, "The intrinsic 'power' by which a person or thing is what it is—the component of a person's or thing's nature that represents its inherent authority."[13]

DOING WHAT COMES NATURALLY

The unique talent—your genius—described by Chopra also comes to you quite naturally. The English dictionary definition of *genius* that fits most closely with my use of the word is "a natural ability or capacity." Your genius is always at the ready, seeking opportunities to manifest itself. It comes with ease. The *Tao Te Ching* states: "Possessing *Teh* is to be serene; with little effort much is done and motives diminish."[14]

Buddhist scholar S. N. Tandon traced the term *dharma* to its origins, concluding that "*dharma* means the natural state or condition of beings and things, what sustains, the law of their being, what is right for them to be, the very stuff of their being."[15]

This natural quality of genius is what makes it so difficult to recognize. We take it for granted. We don't notice it. This is why we struggle to recognize it. It is also why recognizing your genius is so significant for your work and career: wouldn't it be great to be at work and do what comes naturally to you?

Among the people whose stories grace this book, Tia, who calls her genius Taking Care, said, "This is how my soul has chosen to express itself in this lifetime. Knowing this is a big plus. I waste less energy. I focus on what is important in my life. I am more productive."

GUARDIAN AND GUIDE

Plato's *daimon* acts as the guardian for the person it accompanies, and this idea is also reflected in Christian guardian angels. Psalm 91 states, "No evil will befall you, nor will any plague come near your tent. For He will give His angels charge concerning you, to guard you in all your ways."[16]

Genius is, however, not a mere impassive sentinel; it also offers guidance. Somé writes, "We look to the Spirit world for the ultimate helper who assists the individual in fulfilling his or her purpose. . . . Your *siura* is behind you, trying to work with you as closely as possible to keep you on the path of your purpose, speaking to you through your inspiration, your dreams, and your instincts."[17]

William Blake reveals that he also sees genius as a guide to fulfilling his purpose. In a letter to a friend, he writes, "I find more and more that my style of designing is a species by itself, and in this which I send you have been compelled by my genius or angel to follow where he led; if I were to act otherwise it would not fulfill the purpose for which alone I live."[18]

Plato calls the *daimon* "tutelary," suggesting that it is also a guide or a teacher. Socrates experienced his *daimon* as a divine presence that would warn him if he was about to do something foolish.

DANGEROUS IGNORANCE

Blake thought that if he shunned his genius, he would not fulfill the purpose of his life. The Yoruba believe that your *ase* is the power by which you are who you are. Jews teach that finding your special treasure is an obligation. The Dagara believe that failure to find sustenance for your genius kills it and you. Ananda Coomaraswamy, a linguist, philosopher, and art historian, writes, "No man . . . can be a genius; but all men have a genius, to be served or disobeyed at their own peril."[19] Alberto, who calls his genius Discovering Deeper Connections, said, "Whenever I feel like something is missing in my life, what is missing is my genius."

Use **Exercise 4** to examine your understanding of the term genius (see page 124).

Dare we ignore our geniuses? Genius may be thought of as a divine compulsion. A friend told me that he wanted to write a book. "I must do this," he said. "I am convinced this book is inside me and will destroy me if I don't let it out." He said this with a good deal of conviction and passion, and with a hint of desperation as well. Your genius is like my friend's book. It wants to be let out, released to serve the world. It is essential—to the world and to you.

Hillman said it best: "Don't dis the *daimon*."[20]

Your genius is your divine spark, the essence of how you can best express yourself, specifically chosen to guide and protect you. It is a gift to you and your gift to others. It attends you and you alone and is not duplicated anywhere else on the planet. You are responsible for it and to it. It shows up, seeking expression, in everything you do. You must learn to hear and listen to it, to sense its presence in your inclinations, imagination, and dreams. It is your link to the divine.

It is not your purpose; it serves your purpose. It is not your calling, but a power given to you to fulfill your calling. It is not your soul, but the energy of your soul. It is not out there somewhere in the future, but present now. It has always been with you and will always be with you. It will not change, though your understanding of it may grow.

Its reason for being is to serve others merely by being what it is, by nourishing your direction when that direction is worthy, and by alerting you when it is not. You must find others who recognize, cultivate, and treasure it.

Regardless of these lofty and weighty notions, it is your natural power. It comes readily and easily unless you get in its way by ignoring it or dismissing it as insignificant.

Harvest Your Experience

Your self-expression is your gift to the world.
—LAURENCE BOLDT

IN CHAPTER 4, we took a break from the work of helping you recognize your genius in order to deepen our understanding of the very idea that you do, indeed, have a genius and what that means for your work. In this chapter, we will return to helping you recognize your genius by finding a name for it.

Earlier, I described a fertile field of experience in which to search for your genius: **Notice what you do when you are not noticing what you do.** This is a way of examining your current experience. Certain aspects of your past are also fertile fields of experience. You may find your genius in any or all of the following fields of past experience:

- **Refute your disrepute.** When your genius is perceived by others as inconvenient or annoying, they often pin negative labels on you, such as "unable to commit," "flighty," "bossy," "distant," and so on. These labels are your disrepute and offer clues to your genius.

- **Follow your frustration.** Often, when your conscious plans or unconscious agendas seem to be defeated, your genius is being frustrated. Following frustration to its source may reveal your genius.

- **Examine your elation.** Sometimes, elation is a sign that the intent of your genius has been realized.

- **Observe what you offer.** Your genius is a gift in two ways: it is a gift to you and your gift to others. Clues to your genius can be found in the help you offer others.

- **Look into your interests.** Those activities in which you engage mostly for pleasure, whether or not other people are involved, are often the most potent clues to your genius.

- **Study your success**. Your success is often the result of doing what comes naturally to you. You will gain clues to your genius by examining what you brought to situations in which you were successful.

- **Investigate compelling images.** The paintings, photographs, sculptures, and other representations of reality to which you are attracted may be echoes of your genius.

This is not a complete list; you may find your genius elsewhere. It does, however, describe fields in which your genius is likely to be found.

The diagram below illustrates the relationships among the basic process for recognizing your genius, the fields of experience, and the approaches to working with information. The process and approaches were introduced in Chapter 3. You will enter a field of experience by reading, doing the suggested exercises, and generating information about yourself. Then, you will begin to associate different pieces of information that seem somehow to fit together. This should happen spontaneously and also while you are doing the exercises. Finally, you will look beneath the information to find your genius.

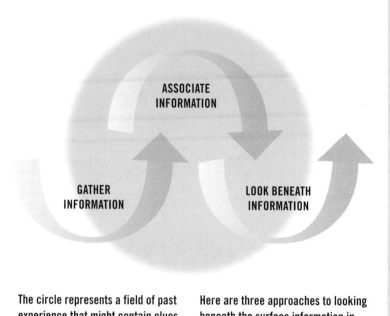

ASSOCIATE
INFORMATION

GATHER
INFORMATION

LOOK BENEATH
INFORMATION

The circle represents a field of past experience that might contain clues to your genius. The fields are

- Refuting your disrepute
- Following your frustration
- Examining your elation
- Observing what you offer
- Looking into your interests
- Studying your success
- Investigating compelling images
- Trusting your intuition

Here are three approaches to looking beneath the surface information in order to recognize your genius:

- Peeling the onion
- Finding the common denominator
- Finding the shared thread of your intent

The fields of past experience in which you might recognize your genius have been tested enough to show that all of them are useful to some people and that none of them is useful to everyone. If any particular field does not seem helpful to you, go on to a different one. Do not expect that any one field will provide you with all the information you need to recognize your genius. That process usually requires an accumulation of information from several fields, and when you reach critical mass of information, the right name for your genius emerges. For example, June began to recognize her genius by noticing something she was doing in the present—taking notes and creating a phone list. She then associated that behavior with her interests—sewing and gardening. Finally, she associated all of that information with the elation she often felt about her new work.

The stories of three people—Neil, Joyce, and Derek—who came to recognize their own geniuses offer good examples of exploring the fields of experience.

FIELDS OF PAST EXPERIENCE

When Neil was very small, he loved to open kitchen cabinets, pull pots and pans out onto the floor, and examine each utensil carefully. After he had emptied a cabinet, he would crawl into it, searching for whatever else might be found within. He also was enchanted by opening and emptying boxes and unpacking grocery bags. His parents described him as "wonderfully curious." They delighted in his craving for discovery. With a large measure of pride, they told their friends and family members, "He's into everything."

Neil's searching didn't stop when childhood ended. He sought new doors to open and new spaces to explore throughout grade school and high school. Drawing, astronomy, NASCAR, baseball, politics, and herbal remedies all drew his attention. His parents encouraged each of his pursuits. When he became interested in the night sky, he asked for and received a telescope. When he became interested in politics, he ran for student council with enthusiastic support from home.

Everything changed during Neil's senior year in high school. Well, not everything—Neil didn't change. He was college bound, people thought, and with a bright future. Neil's father was a lawyer, but neither of his parents pushed Neil toward any particular decision about a prospective career. They did, however, push him to make decisions about his future. What major would he pursue? What was the best college for that major? Neil resisted making those decisions. He read every college catalogue he could get his hands on and wanted to visit every college that seemed even mildly interesting. He couldn't understand why his parents or a college would want him to decide on a major course of study. His attitude seemed to be, Why can't I just go somewhere, walk into classrooms, see what's going on, and find what interests me?

During that year, Neil's approach to deciding on a college became increasingly more annoying to his parents and his guidance counselor. The small child who was once viewed as "wonderfully curious" had become an "unfocused," "disorganized" teenager who "lacked direction" and was "unable to commit." He, in turn, was frustrated and angered by the reactions of the adults around him, who he felt had betrayed him in some way that he couldn't identify.

Neil did not enter college immediately after high school. He stayed at home, worked odd jobs, and took a few courses: one in drawing at an art school, two in business at a community college. At twenty-one, he left the midsize town where he had grown up and moved to the nearest big city—Chicago.

Twenty-five years later, Neil attended a weekend workshop in which he and fourteen other people received guidance on recognizing their geniuses. He was the CEO of his own very successful high-end travel-planning and adventure guide business. The wonderfully curious child who became a maddeningly curious teenager had grown into a successfully curious adult. During his years in Chicago, he completed a degree in business administration and started and sold two other businesses. He had traveled extensively in South America, Asia, and Europe. He had also written and published several travel-related articles.

Refuting Your Disrepute

Neil's story illustrates how refuting your disrepute can offer clues to your genius. Our strengths are very easily seen as weaknesses by others for whom those traits become inconvenient or annoying. For example, extroverted people are sometimes seen as dominating whatever group of people they are with, and those who are good at planning are sometimes seen as impeding the progress of others who are ready to move beyond planning and into action. So the characteristics that others consider weaknesses may hold clues to your genius.

References to those so-called weaknesses are usually expressed in negative terms, like those assigned to Neil during his senior year. The behavior and attitudes that produce those negative labels are what I mean when I speak of "disrepute." When we become annoying and inconvenient to others, their first tendency usually is to assign a negative label to us. The spirit in Neil that gave rise to those negative labels was the same spirit that made him seem "wonderfully curious" as a child and was encouraged and enjoyed by those around him until his senior year. It was a spirit of seemingly unquenchable curiosity.

Negative labels that have been assigned to you by others are powerful clues to your genius if you can answer this question: What is it about me that was annoying or inconvenient to the person who assigned the label to me? The most important negative labels to explore are those that hurt you and have stayed with you. You remember them because they wounded your spirit.

During the workshop, Neil talked about the negative labels that had been assigned to him in his senior year. They seemed to be important clues to his genius, but a name for it eluded him until he recalled one other area of disrepute, another negative label. This label surfaced yearly during holiday gatherings when his family watched home movies of him and his younger brother. One, a family favorite, shows Neil in the distance, at age eight, standing next to his six-year-old brother on a deserted beach. Neil gesticulates energetically and points off camera into the distance. Whenever the film was shown, one or the other of Neil's parents would mention how "bossy" Neil had always been.

When Neil told the other people in the workshop about this negative label, he explained, "I wasn't trying to boss my brother around. I was inviting him to come with me and explore another section of the beach. I wanted him to be as excited about exploring the beach as I was."

Use **Exercise 5** to refute your disrepute for clues to your genius (see page 125).

This statement provided the key that led Neil to recognize his genius. He calls it Exploring Pathways. As a small child, he had thought of each closed cabinet, each box, and each grocery bag as a pathway. Next, music, astronomy, NASCAR, baseball, politics, and herbal remedies became pathways to explore. Then Chicago. And then the two businesses he started and sold before he opened his travel-planning and adventure guide business. The current business seems perfect for Neil; it allows him to explore ever new pathways in countries all over the world.

Following Your Frustration

Neil's story is also a good example of how following your frustration offers clues to your genius. His experience in senior year with his parents and guidance counselor was just as frustrating for him as it was for them: he wanted every opportunity to explore pathways, while they wanted a decision about a single course of action.

Frustration occurs when it seems that your conscious plans or unconscious agendas are being thwarted. You feel baffled and, perhaps, useless. Frustration visits you when what you are trying to do isn't working. Hans Selye, who is best known for his research and writing about stress, says,

> Blocking the fulfillment of man's natural drives causes as much distress as the forced prolongation and intensification of any activity beyond the desired level. Ignoring this rule leads to frustration, fatigue, and exhaustion which can progress to a mental or physical breakdown.[1]

If you notice your frustration early, before it progresses to the fatigue, exhaustion, and breakdown that Selye describes, you may gain valuable clues about your genius by following your frustration to its source.

When you feel frustrated, ask, "What about me is being frustrated?" It is a different approach to frustration. We usually attribute our frustration to something outside ourselves: he frustrates me, she frustrates me, or it frustrates me. Asking this question will force you to look within yourself for your genius. The usual way of viewing Neil's frustration would lead us to conclude that it was caused by the expectations of those around him who wanted him to make a decision. But by asking, "What about me is being frustrated?" Neil could see his genius—Exploring Pathways.

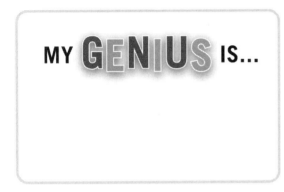

MY GENIUS IS...

Joyce's experience in her marriage also illustrates that your frustration may be a clue to your genius. It also shows how your genius is alive in other aspects of your life, not just in your work and career.

Joyce and her husband had been married for twenty years. Her genius is Digging Deeper. Here is how she described it: "When I get involved in something, I really sink myself into it. I want to be part of everything there is to do with it, the big picture, the meaning of the whole thing, the details, the day-to-day of it, everything. I think about whatever it is constantly. I want to talk about it all the time, and I want, always, to find some deeper meaning for what is happening. I get totally involved. Whatever it is becomes like a religion for me."

Joyce's attempts to dig deeper into the problems in her marriage created years of frustration for her. While Joyce would have liked to spend a weekend at a couples' retreat, her husband would have preferred a weekend at a resort with a great golf course. His attitude, Joyce reported, was, "I'd rather live my life than discuss it."

If we looked at Joyce's frustration in the usual way, we would say that Joyce's husband was the source of her frustration. But Joyce asked instead what about her was being frustrated. She said, "The problem was that I wanted to dig deeper into the marriage and my husband wouldn't."

Joyce rented an apartment and lived alone for six months. She felt she needed to take that step so that she could learn about herself.

Use **Exercise 6** to follow your frustration for clues to your genius. (see page 126).

After her six-month hiatus, Joyce chose to remain in her marriage. She said, "When I focused on digging deeply first and foremost in myself, the problems I was having with my marriage went away. I could be who I am—someone constantly digging deeper—and allow my husband to be who he is."

Frustration is not always a clue to your genius, however. For example, you may also feel frustration when learning a new skill. That frustration may or may not provide clues to your genius.

Examining Your Elation

Your elation also may contain clues to your genius. I am referring not to the elation related to seemingly chance events such as winning the lottery but to the elation that accompanies the sense of "I did it!" This variety of elation lies in the opposite direction from your frustration. Frustration arises when the agenda of your genius is frustrated. Elation arises when that agenda is realized and you are successful, when you have fulfilled the intent of your genius.

Use **Exercise 7** to examine your elation for clues to your genius (see page 127).

In order to recognize your genius within your elation, ask yourself, "What is it about me that is being fulfilled?"

Observing What You Offer

Neil recognized his genius in his invitation to his brother to explore the beach. He was offering his genius to his brother. As a business owner, he continues to offer his genius to his customers. Joyce left books about relationships and brochures advertising couples' retreats lying around the house in the hope that her husband would become interested in digging deeper into their marriage. Each book and brochure was an offering that hinted at her genius.

In Christian and Jewish thought, in Chinese and West African faiths, in the beliefs of ancient Greece and Rome, and everywhere else that the concept of genius is found, it contains this idea: your genius is the gift you have been given so that you might offer it to others.

Use **Exercise 8** to observe what you offer for clues to your genius (see page 128).

In order to observe what you offer, ask yourself these questions: "What is it that I consistently attempt to give to others?" and "What is it that others seek when they come to me for help?" If you want to be brave, and if you know people who will understand what you are seeking, ask them, "What do you come to me for?" These questions must be asked and answered on an abstract rather than a concrete level. For example, Joyce asked her teenage son what he wants when he comes to her. He looked puzzled for a moment, as if he were being tested, and then answered uncertainly, "Money?" Clearly, this sort of answer would not help in identifying your genius.

Looking into Your Interests

Although I love hooking and landing a good fish, I don't much mind coming home with an empty creel as long as I have had a good time. A good time means that I have been actively working at something I really enjoy. I enjoy creating clarity about the business of fishing for trout on a particular stretch of a particular river under the conditions of a particular day. Creating that clarity is more important to me than hooking and landing a trout. My intent is not so much to hook a fish as it is to engage my genius in creating clarity about hooking a fish.

Your genius is present in activities that you do solely for yourself, even when other people are not involved. You can find clues to your genius in such activities by inspecting your intentions. Your intention is your "going in" agenda, the contribution your genius attempts to supply when it is switched on.

The story of Derek recognizing his genius illustrates how genius reveals itself in your interests and may be identified by seeking a shared thread of intent among them. Derek is a minister who invited me to speak about genius to his congregation. We agreed before the event that he would participate in a demonstration during which we would attempt to find a name for his genius.

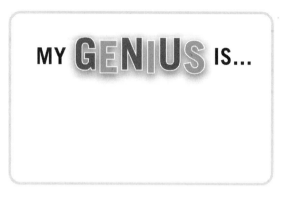

As we stood together before his congregation, I asked him to tell me about activities that he enjoys, that seem to come naturally to him, and that bring him a sense of success. Your genius is likely to be very active in activities that meet those three criteria. Derek told of the joy he experiences in building his congregation one person at a time. He is very good at this; his congregation is large. He also told of two interests: discovering new ideas and collecting stamps.

When Derek spoke of building his congregation, he repeatedly moved his hands and arms with a motion that reminded me of someone trying to get his arms around a tree trunk, almost a hugging motion. Gestures often provide clues to genius, as if the genius is expressing itself through the body. I asked Derek to perform the gesture repeatedly until he could put words to it.

Repeating the motion with his arms, he said, "Gathering. I'm gathering something. In this case, gathering people."

Referring to the other activities Derek had mentioned, I asked, "And do you also gather ideas and stamps? Does your genius have something to do with gathering?"

"Yes. Of course," he said, with obvious delight.

Then I asked, "What is the shared thread of your intent in the people, ideas, and stamps that you gather? What do those things have in common in your mind?"

He said that he collected American stamps of the early 1900s, especially commemorative stamps, because, in his words, "I have

Use **Exercise 9** to look into your interests for clues to your genius (see page 129).

always been fascinated by that period in history, and I love how the stamps capture the spirit of the time." I asked him to talk about his other interest, about the ideas he most enjoys exploring. He replied that he reads many spiritually oriented books, looking for ideas that resonate with him.

Derek did not see the shared thread of intent yet, but it was becoming apparent. He gathered people for spiritual purposes. He gathered spiritual ideas. He gathered stamps that reveal the spirit of the early 1900s.

I took a stab at it and asked, "Is your genius Gathering Spirit?"

Derek's face showed the glow of delight and surprise that often accompanies the moment of recognizing one's genius. He repeated the words slowly, in wonderment. "Gathering Spirit. Yes," he said, "my genius is Gathering Spirit."

Derek's conscious intent was to bring people into his congregation, to discover ideas that deepen his spirituality, and to collect stamps that reveal the tone of an era. But the underlying shared thread of intent in all of those activities is gathering spirit.

Studying Your Success

Many of your moments or periods of success occur when your genius is operating at full throttle in situations that call for it and when it is valued by the other people involved. In other words, your success is often the result of doing what comes naturally to you in a supportive atmosphere and where you are truly needed.

Use **Exercise 10** to study your success for clues to your genius (see page 130).

Both Derek and Neil are able to bring their geniuses to their work, and both are surrounded by people who value what they bring to their work. Derek is well loved among the congregation he has so successfully built, and Neil's business thrives.

You will find clues to your genius by asking yourself, "What did I bring to the situations in which I was most successful?" Again, look for the common denominator among your moments or periods of success.

Investigating Compelling Images

Neil likes maps; they illustrate pathways. Joyce has reproductions of pottery excavated from Native American ruins; they are the results of digging. One of my favorite sculptures is Rodin's *The Thinker*, which took inspiration from imagining Dante, seated before the Gates of Hell, contemplating his epic poem. To me, the figure depicts a man creating clarity.

Images that compel are potent gateways to your genius because genius lies closer to the soul, which transacts its business in images, than to the mind, which deals in words and thoughts.

Use **Exercise 11** to investigate compelling images for clues to your genius (see page 134).

Take note of the images that compel you. In particular, notice images of people—photographs, paintings, drawings, sculpture. Can you identify with any of the people in the images? What are they doing? What do you think they are getting out of their activities? What are they doing that other people would appreciate? In what way do you identify with them? The answers to those questions may contain hints about your genius.

Trusting Your Intuition

Neil, Joyce, and Derek came to recognize their geniuses through different methods: Neil by refuting the disrepute of being labeled with such terms as "lacking direction" and "bossy," Joyce by examining the source of her frustration, and Derek by seeking the shared thread of intent among activities that he enjoys. But recognition of your genius may not be as direct and clear as it was in those three examples. Genius often eludes recognition even after you have examined the field of current experience and one or more of the fields of past experience.

Trusting your intuition is also an important part of naming your genius. Here is what I mean: I'm sitting at my word processor, thinking about what I want to say, and getting the words out. I stop for a moment, and a seemingly extraneous thought enters my mind. One way of dealing with that thought is to banish it. A second way is to ask myself, "I wonder what that thought has to do with my writing?" Sometimes, the thought is in fact entirely extraneous—for example, "I forgot to pick up the laundry"—but often the thought leads me into an area I need to explore in my writing.

As you seek a name for your genius, trust those seemingly extraneous thoughts long enough to find out what they mean. Ask, "What does this thought have to do with my genius?" These thoughts will most likely come to you during a break in the conscious work of discovering a name.

Exercises 12 and 13 also contain strategies for recognizing your genius (see pages 136 and 138).

Alberto's experience is a good example of how getting away from the conscious work of naming your genius can be productive. He said, "One evening I examined stories about frustration and my disrepute, but the information just sat there, and I wasn't able to bring any focus to it. The next morning, I went for a run. When I run, I like to let my imagination wander. I remember vividly, although it has been almost fifteen years, the place where I was when the words that describe my genius—Discovering Deeper Connections—seemed to come out of nowhere and hit me. Those words crystallized something that is essentially me."

The methods that have been described thus far, and those in the exercises at the back of this book, are not always sure paths to recognizing your genius. They may provide only hints, or even contradictory suggestions, about your genius. If that happens, you will have to go one step further, treating all of the bits of information gathered from the various methods and exercises as pieces of a larger puzzle. Solving that puzzle is the subject of the next chapter.

Pursue the
Blinding Flash

*The orderly and wise soul follows its guide
and understands its circumstances.*

—PLATO

MOST PEOPLE WHO have recognized their genius recall vividly the moment in which recognition occurred. The recognition and a name arrive in a flash, an Aha! that is at the same time blinding in its perfection and obvious in its rightness.

Tia's moment was quite dramatic. She is a colleague of mine who had practiced noticing what she is doing when she is not noticing what she is doing. She had followed her frustration. And she had talked to several people who knew her well. She named her genius Taking Charge and told me that the name seemed to fit her. Tia is wonderful at organizing. When she leads a workshop, she looks to see what needs to be done and then she does it. When we work together, if I say, "We need to get this done by Friday. Can you take care of it?" I know that if she agrees, it surely will be done by Friday.

But something nagged at Tia. She told me, "The name Taking Charge feels pretty good, but I don't get excited about it. It is true about me, but I sense that I'm missing something. I'm still thinking about it, and I don't know why." If you have arrived at a name for your genius but have nagging doubts about it, I urge you to trust those doubts and keep on searching for a name.

Tia and I talked about her discomfort. She expressed surprise about something a friend had told her, that he admires the way she takes care of herself. She said, "I was surprised to hear this remark. I never thought about taking care of myself. But when I examined it, I realized that I do. I take great care of myself. I limited my traveling because it was too stressful. I work out regularly. I get my hair and nails done every week whether I need to or not. I put those things on my calendar and give them priority. I get help when I need it. When I wanted to spend more time at home, I gave up my office space and moved everything to my house."

I said, "Maybe your genius is Taking Care rather than Taking Charge."

Tia is not given to overt displays of emotion, but at that moment, she began to cry.

Later, she described the experience. "You talk about gut feelings!" she told me. "When you said 'Taking Care,' something just bubbled up inside me. It started somewhere in my gut and came straight up. What an emotional release! Taking Care just felt so right, and I felt so relieved to know myself in that way. It was wonderful. In that instant, I truly saw myself. I saw my own energy and power."

Tia's experience of naming her genius is instructive in three ways. First, her reaction when she heard the words "Taking Care" is one of the more dramatic examples of what I call the **moment of recognition**; it was truly a blinding flash. What happened inside Tia at that moment was a knowing that goes beyond intellectual knowledge. It involved her whole self—her body, mind, feeling, and spirit. It was a felt sense of rightness.

I can usually tell when another person has truly discovered his or her genius because the person's response to the discovery is physical. It isn't always as dramatic as Tia's tears. Sometimes, it shows as a grin or a smile, the kind of smile that says, "Oh my! Yes! That's it! And isn't it great!" One person described the feeling as a "buzz."

The experience might also be anxiety or fear. Joyce, whose genius is Digging Deeper, said, "When I started to get close to my moment of discovery, I didn't want my genius to be Digging Deeper. A friend talked it through with me and heard how upset I was. Finally, it clicked that this is it. Some part of me didn't want to see it or was afraid of it."

The second significant aspect of Tia's experience is that the name Taking Care was not the first name she thought of for her genius. This is often the case. As explained earlier, the process of naming your genius is like peeling an onion. The outer layers usually consist of skills, talents, interests, or abilities you developed to give a voice to your genius. Tia's ability to take charge and her skills at organization are the mechanisms her genius uses to express itself. Her primary intent when she is taking charge or organizing is taking care.

When I was trying to name my genius, I thought of Creating Learning Experiences, Putting Ideas Together, and Seeking Truth as possible names but did not experience a felt sense of rightness about them. Yes, I do all of those things, but I only do them in the service of creating clarity. Those are skills, talents, interests, and abilities that form the outer layers of the onion; they are not the common thread of my intent.

The only true test of the rightness of your chosen name lies in your felt sense of its rightness. When it is right, you will know it. Remember, however, that sometimes a genius makes itself difficult to name. If your genius is something like Considering Alternatives or Going Deeper, you will probably find a name and then want to think about alternatives or peel the onion further.

The third important aspect of Tia's moment of discovery is that she talked with other people about her genius. She used the feedback she got from others to help in her search. The friend who told her that he admired the way she takes care of herself gave Tia a wonderful gift—the missing clue to her genius. And when she spoke of her discomfort, she alerted me to the need to look for further clues, to help her discover her thread of intent, and to notice that her genius was contained in the very words her friend had spoken to her.

The people who know you often see aspects of you that you do not see yourself. This is particularly true of your genius, which comes so naturally to you that you may take it for granted and not notice it. Joyce said, "It's so much a part of the fabric of who I am that I couldn't see it. It was invisible to me because I experienced it as a universal thing that everybody did."

Dan also got an important clue from other people. He was attending a workshop that included recognizing genius as part of a larger agenda. The workshop contained free time for reflection, journal writing, and recreation. During one of these periods, Dan and a few others decided to rent a sailboat and sail across a nearby lake. Dan, an accomplished sailor, asked the others, "Where do you want to go?" They told him, and they set off, with Dan taking on the role of figuring out how to get to their chosen destination. Over dinner that evening, the group talked excitedly about the experience. One of Dan's fellow sailors noted, "Dan was more interested in charting the course than in actually sailing the boat."

Dan heard the words "charting the course" and knew instantly that he had found his genius. He described this moment of discovery as "a jolt." He recognized immediately how he goes about charting the course at work, in his family life, and in his career.

MAKING IT WORK

Sometimes, genius reveals itself very slowly and in stages, with several lesser moments of recognition spread out over the course of months or even years before a blinding flash occurs. Alicia, the training manager for a large corporation, peeled back the onion to reveal her genius over a period of five years. She began during a workshop, when she first named her genius Opening Doors.

"The name Opening Doors came mostly from the work I do," she said. "I liked putting ideas or activities on the table when I thought they had the potential to change something in somebody's life. My thrill was in making the opportunities available to other people. I didn't have an enormous need for people to embrace what I was offering. I merely wanted to open doors so that they could see things in new ways and could grow. It was like planting seeds that other people would have to nurture."

Alicia was nagged by the thought that the name Opening Doors was not quite right, that there was something more, something she could not quite grasp.

"Opening Doors did not account for how deeply I commit myself to whatever I'm doing and the passion I bring to the things I am involved in," she said. "For example, I'm never merely a member of the professional associations I join; I'm a board member, president, or committee chairperson. In my personal life, when my kids went to nursery school, I volunteered one day a week."

About a year after the workshop, Alicia took the name Immersing Myself for her genius. She had noticed that she was trying very hard to get her colleagues at work to feel the same enthusiasm she felt for an upcoming project although they resisted becoming excited about it. She viewed her frustration over not being able to engage them as a clue that Opening Doors was not precisely the right name for her genius. She had to peel the onion further.

She said, "When I thought of the name Immersing Myself, it did more to explain the pain I felt over not being able to get my colleagues engaged. Opening Doors did not explain my frustration about that, and the name just felt more and more hollow to me."

Alicia used the name Immersing Myself to describe her genius over the next four years. "I still see a lot of truth in that name," she said. "But I noticed that I had become involved with lots of things without immersing myself. I also noticed that I am not a detail person except when the issue I am working on is important to me and there is no one else to attend to the details. Then I will handle the details, but it's under duress."

Alicia decided to change jobs, and during the year following that decision, she came to a new understanding of her genius. "I realized, when explaining my job change to people, that I kept saying over and over again, 'I just couldn't make it work.' Then I started thinking that my genius is Making It Work. It isn't enough for me to be a casual observer of things I care about. I go into fix-it mode."

Alicia believes this description of her genius fits snugly. "I was drawn to my profession so that I could find resources to apply to situations that don't work. Making It Work explains my work very well. It also explains how I have always been with my kids, my husband, and other significant people in my life. Opening doors and immersing myself are simply strategies I use in the process of making it work."

Alicia's five-year exploration of her genius is not unusual. Many people find a name that fits and keep it. Others find new depths of meaning under the first names they choose. The genius has not changed, only the depth of understanding, and we gain an awareness that what we at first took for genius was not genius at all but a learned skill or strategy—an outer layer of the onion.

SEARCHING TOGETHER

The blinding flash of recognition often comes during dialogue with other people, as Tia's did. The remainder of this chapter tells part of the story of a group of people who helped one another to recognize their geniuses. The story illustrates the way in which the pieces of a person's puzzle may come together to reveal a picture of genius, the value of feedback and dialogue, and how the moment of recognition often feels. It also offers a sense of what it is like to be in such a group and explores what you can do to help another person recognize his or her genius.

We sat in a circle in a softly lit oak-paneled room, sixteen people, including me. Through large windows, we saw snow falling gently on brittle grass and frozen earth. All of the other people worked for the same company. They were present to recognize their geniuses, and I was present as their guide. It was a Sunday afternoon, near the end of our get-together; we had been at work since Saturday morning.

In the time since our arrival, we had talked about genius and about noticing, frustration, disrepute, and intent. They had told many stories about themselves and had created lists of words that might provide clues to recognizing genius. They all had many pieces of their individual puzzles.

Those who had found names for their geniuses wore tags displaying the names. Mine said Creating Clarity. The name tags were used, as they are in this book, as a device to encourage people to name their genius and also to help us determine how far we had to go yet before everyone felt satisfied.

At the beginning of each session, those who had changed their name tags since the last session were invited to talk about the new names they had found.

Frank, a midlevel manager who was not wearing a name tag, told of his struggle to find the right name. He said that he seemed to be getting nowhere. With a chuckle, he remarked, "I'm beginning to think my genius is Avoiding Myself."

Sam worked in maintenance. His name tag read Talking It Out, but he told us that he thought the name was not quite right. He said he wanted more help from the group before we finished.

Carmen was an administrative assistant. She also said that she wanted to talk more about her genius. Her name tag read Developing Hope.

Ann, a training manager, spoke first: "Why is this so tough? If my genius is so natural to my being, why can't I find it? It seems like it shouldn't be this hard."

Ann was correct. It seems like it shouldn't be hard, but often it is. Although naming your genius simply means recognizing a natural aspect of yourself, it can be a challenge.

Feeling Deeply

Ann admitted, "I'm so frustrated by the invisibility of my genius."

Frank said, "What I notice about you, Ann, is that you really seem to connect with other people's emotions. You look sad when someone else is having a tough time, and you smile easily when someone else is laughing about something. When I was frustrated yesterday, you seemed to understand it completely."

The people in this group have learned that sharing what they notice about one another in a nonjudgmental way is a powerful favor.

"I do," Ann replied. "That's why I think my genius has something to do with other people."

"What is your unique way of helping?" I asked.

By definition, genius is an offering to other people, so saying that your genius is helping is like saying that your genius is your genius; it does not add to your understanding. The question to ask is, What is my unique offering? I wanted Ann to see that she helps others in ways that she helps herself, and that her way of helping is hers alone.

She seemed puzzled by the question.

Trusting a hunch, I then invited Ann to follow her frustration. "What is it about you that is being frustrated right now?" I asked.

"I don't know. I can't get at it," she replied. "But while Frank was talking about how I connect with other people's feelings, I thought of my former career. I used to work as a nurse. I got out because it was tearing me apart."

Ann was paying attention to a seemingly extraneous thought about her nursing career. Such thoughts are often important clues about genius.

"How was it tearing you apart?" I asked.

Ann suddenly looked shocked. Her face crumbled. She leaned over, hiding her face in her hands. Her shoulders shook. She was crying.

"You just got it, didn't you?" I said to her.

She sat up again, tears still flowing down her cheeks.

"Yes," she replied softly, "my genius is Feeling Deeply. I'm always the one who cries or laughs the most, feels the most frustrated or the angriest. That's why I had to leave nursing. I truly believe that I felt other people's pain. It was too much pain for me."

The room was quiet, all eyes on Ann, as a smile began to glimmer through her tears. She sat back, relaxed, breathed a sigh, and then began laughing.

"It's been there all along, but because it caused me so much pain when I was a nurse, I think I tried to push it away." Then she exclaimed, "God! It felt good to cry!"

The rest of us burst into laughter. Ann had not only told us about her genius but also allowed us to see it in action. She cries easily, and laughs easily, because she feels deeply.

When the laughter ended, I asked, "Who's next?"

Searching for Clues

Stan, whose name tag read "Building Bridges," said to Frank, "You amaze me. You notice everything. You're often the one who provides other people with the right clues. Like what you said to Ann about how she reads other people's feelings. Could that have something to do with your genius?" Building bridges is about forming connections, and Stan had just connected Frank's genius with Frank's comments to Ann.

Frank looked puzzled, as if he did not recognize this about himself. Other people nodded their heads to affirm Stan's observation.

"My wife often tells me, 'You don't miss a trick,'" Frank said. He also added, in a quiet aside to the person sitting next to him, "I don't have a clue."

Such asides, which I call "throwaways," often are significant clues to a person's genius. I began to wonder if Frank's genius has something to do with clues.

Ann asked, "What are your hobbies, Frank?"

"I photograph wildlife," he replied. "I like searching the woods for clues—tracking. The photography is really kind of secondary; it's proof that I found what I was looking for."

I had another hunch. "Could your genius be something like Searching for Clues?" I asked. Frank looked directly at me, and his eyes grew wide. I thought I was on to something, but I knew Frank had to arrive at his genius himself. I would explain my hunch but not try to convince him of its validity. It is crucial in these sessions to allow people to arrive at their own conclusions.

"You search for clues about wildlife in the woods. You've been searching for clues about other people's geniuses. It appears that you want others to have the gift of your clues."

I also know that these observations are outward manifestations of Frank's genius, so I asked, "Do you search for clues about yourself?"

"With a vengeance," he replied. "I read everything about self-help. I do all the exercises in all the books. I'm here at this workshop looking for clues about myself."

Frank's smile was wide, and I knew he had arrived at his moment of recognition. He reached for a name tag and wrote on it "Searching for Clues."

Finding the Positive

Carmen's name tag read "Developing Hope." She said, "This name is close but not right."

The group members had told stories to one another about the times when they were successful and things just seemed to flow. I asked her, "What did you notice as common threads from your stories?"

She looked at her notes and said, "When I told my stories, I talked about leading, about identifying opportunities, about developing people and ideas, making a contribution, and taking chances."

"Those are all hopeful concepts," Ann said.

Carmen replied, "I've been thinking that my genius has something to do with hope, but I'm not sure."

Ann asked her to elaborate.

"I always try to see the positive in people and situations. I get frustrated with my husband when he's feeling down. I try to get him to look on the bright side, to be hopeful and see the positive. But sometimes he just wants to vent."

Carmen's frustration with her husband was a clue to her genius. She wanted him to feel hopeful, but he wanted to vent.

She said, "Hope isn't the right concept. I just want to be able to see the positive wherever it exists. Maybe my genius is Seeing the Positive."

I asked her to pick someone in the group, look that person in the eye, and say, "My genius is Seeing the Positive." Announcing your genius in this way, directly to another person, is a way of taking ownership of the name you have found. It is often a difficult thing to do.

Carmen picked Ann. We watched Carmen's reaction as she said the words. "My genius is Seeing the Positive." She looked dubious and uncertain. When she finished speaking, she pursed her lips and shook her head from side to side.

"No," she said. "That's not quite right."

Carmen had not yet found the felt sense of her genius. There was no Aha! No blinding flash. The name wasn't right. "What's wrong with it?" I asked.

"The concept of seeing is too passive," she replied. "I do more than simply see. Sometimes the positive is right in front of me, but sometimes I have to find it, because it isn't obvious."

"So is it Finding the Positive rather than Seeing the Positive?" Ann asked.

"That's it! That's it! Finding the Positive!" Carmen smiled broadly. She was also bouncing up and down lightly in her chair in a way that showed that she had the felt sense of her genius. The blinding flash had occurred.

I asked her, "Will you turn once again to Ann and say, 'My genius is Finding the Positive'?"

Carmen faced Ann and said, "My genius is Finding the Positive."

She said it firmly, with conviction, and everybody, including Carmen, knew that she had recognized her genius.

Generating Warmth

I turned my attention to Sam, who had asked for more time. His name tag read "Talking It Out." He removed it.

"I know this name isn't right," he said. "It looks right, because here I am talking it out again. But there's something underneath—another layer of the onion. I don't think Talking It Out expresses my intent, but I don't know what my intent is."

Because your genius is a gift that you try to give to other people, what other people get from you is often an important clue. For example, I am trying to give you clarity about your genius, and my genius is Creating Clarity.

"What gift do you get from Sam?" I asked the group.

Someone answered immediately. "Warmth," he said. There was a chorus of "yes" from the rest of the group.

Appendix B contains guidelines for groups of people who want to meet for the purpose of recognizing their geniuses (see page 181).

"Well, that's why I like to talk things out with people," Sam said. "I like the warm feeling it creates between us. Sometimes, it doesn't matter what we're talking about, as long as I get that feeling."

"Do you have other ways of creating warmth?" I asked.

"Not Creating Warmth," he replied. "It's Generating Warmth. That's better." A huge grin spread across Sam's face.

I have to be careful. My genius is Creating Clarity, so I often use the word *creating* in my hunches about another person's genius. When you are trying to help someone to recognize his or her genius, remember that you are probably projecting your own genius onto that person.

Returning to my question about other ways of generating warmth, Sam said, "I like to give presents for no special reason. It makes me feel warm. I like getting presents too. I also enjoy calling friends just to say hello. You should see my phone bill." Then he laughed and explained, "This is embarrassing, but in my house, I have a gas heater, electric backup heat, a fireplace, and a kerosene heater for emergencies. I guess generating warmth is pretty important to me."

Sam reached for a new name tag. He wrote "Generating Warmth."

Later, he said about his work, "I was once in a job at which I was a complete failure. For years, I thought it was because there was something wrong with me. When I understood my genius, I could see that the job was, quite simply, the wrong one for me. It didn't engage what is special about me."

Pursuing Understanding

Martin, one of the senior technical people in the plant, was wearing a name tag that read "Solving Problems." He had not asked for time to talk further about his genius, but he said, "I know this name isn't right."

While Solving Problems may very well describe someone's genius, Martin had not peeled the onion enough. Solving problems can be thought of as a set of learned skills rather than a unique natural power.

I invited him to peel the onion further. "We are all in some way problem solvers," I told him. "I wonder what is unique about your way of solving problems. I also wonder if that uniqueness doesn't enact itself in your life in other ways besides problem solving."

"What is it you do when you solve problems?" Frank asked.

Martin replied, "I get involved in as much as I can about the problem. I read about it. I talk to as many people as I can. I surf the Internet. I take copious notes. I think about it incessantly. I take long walks to ruminate. That's for the big problems, but I also love the small ones, like how to organize my closet, or where to put the grill on the deck. I've loved solving the problem of other people's geniuses in this workshop."

Frank had, in fact, been very active in trying to help others recognize their geniuses.

Then he said, "I just had a thought! The problems are like a medium for me, like canvas is to a painter or paper to a writer."

"Do you paint or write?" I asked.

"I used to do both," he replied. "I haven't for some time."

"What did you enjoy about painting and writing?"

"They start with ignorance," he said. "When I painted and wrote, I started with the idea that there was something I didn't know, something I was ignorant about, something I wanted to understand. The painting and writing were my ways of pursuing that understanding."

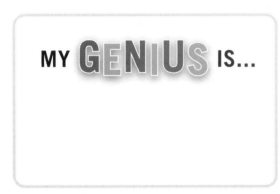

Frank chimed in, "Could your genius be something like Pursuing Understanding?"

"Yes," Martin said softly. The room was quiet as we watched him gaze into space. Martin's moment of recognition was not as overtly dramatic as some others had been, but he seemed certain. A blinding flash can also arrive with a hush.

"Yes," he repeated. "That's what the problem solving is about too. And that's why I've thoroughly enjoyed this process of naming my genius."

IS YOUR GENIUS AT WORK?

Up to this point, I have focused on approaches and strategies that will help you answer the first of the four key questions: What is your genius? Now I will focus briefly on the second question: Is your genius at work?

The second question can be treated briefly because the answer will usually arrive almost immediately after you recognize your genius. For example, Dave, whose genius is Straightening Up, realized that he was uneasy about his first managerial role because he had straightened up the mess he had found when he took the job. He also understood that his decision to move from a technical role to a managerial one was not a mistake as long as he pursued assignments that required straightening up.

Dan, whose genius is Charting the Course, found that his genius was at work in his current job and uncovered the reason he had been successful in some of his previous jobs but not in others.

Use **Exercises 14 and 15** to examine the degree to which your genius is at work in your current job (see pages 142 and 144).

Dan is a manager, but he is not particularly visionary. If asked to manage a group that has a clear vision, however, he will chart the course to its achievement.

Neil's genius is Exploring Pathways. He understood right away after recognizing his genius that running his travel and adventure business is perfect for him. He also understood why he sometimes appears directionless to others, having started and sold previous businesses as well as explored seemingly extraneous pathways such as drawing and writing. He resolved to explain to the important people in his life why he appears directionless and to not be troubled if his explanations were disregarded.

And when Francine recognized her genius—Engaging the Heart—it clarified her reasons for being unhappy in her job and indicated what she needed to find in her next one.

Use **Exercise 16** to describe how you add value to work that you pursue (see page 146).

So it is quite likely that after recognizing your genius, you will have an immediate answer to the question "Is your genius at work?" It is also likely that you will find hints about what to do. The degree to which your genius is at work in your current job and the degree of work satisfaction that you are now experiencing will probably match each other closely.

You have three options you might pursue if your genius is not now at work in a significant way. First, you can resign yourself to the situation. Many people express good reasons for doing so, mostly related to economic security. If you choose this option, take care to find other means for your genius to express itself, such as hobbies or volunteer work. And start now to plan for a day when you no longer must resign yourself to an unsatisfactory situation.

Second, you might attempt to reshape your job. For example, after Dave discovered the source of his unhappiness, he spoke with his boss, explaining what he had discovered about himself. His boss was delighted to find Dave a new situation that needed straightening up. Sometimes, the solution is even simpler, and just a slight shift in responsibilities is all that is needed.

Use **Exercise 17** to discover the conditions under which your genius thrives (see page 147).

The third option is to make a more far-reaching change. It might be a change such as Francine's, finding a new place to do the work she has trained herself to do. Or it could be something more drastic, such as setting out on an entirely new career path, with all of the effort, study, worry, and excitement that a new path entails.

When you have recognized your genius, you will be able to pursue whatever option you choose with a stronger sense of your value and with greater confidence.

Detect Your Purpose

My business is circumference.

—EMILY DICKINSON

IN MARION ZIMMER BRADLEY'S novel *The Mists of Avalon,* the knight Lancelot says of his quest for the Holy Grail, "It was as if a great bell called to me, far away, a light like to the faraway lights in the marsh, saying, 'Follow.'"[1]

The line is a marvelous description of the awareness reported by those who experience a clear sense of purpose in their lives. A black teenage mother, homeless in a ghetto, promised a benefactor that she would do for others what the benefactor did for her. Thirty years later, she was honored with a state government award for her charitable work in the community. A singer for a band prodded her eight-year-old son to lead the band when the rightful leader was absent. The boy became an honored orchestra conductor. An aimless young man discovered the joys of pottery and made it his life's work to bring the artistry that had been his salvation to others. These are people who, like Lancelot, heard the call of a "great bell." But don't be deceived by these three brief vignettes into believing that the bell calls only to the young. The story of Michael Azzopardi's purpose literally arriving at his doorstep when he was in his fifties provides a rich example of a calling. His story will be told later in this chapter.

We have reached the point of asking the third of the four key questions that were posed in Chapter 1: What is your purpose?

THE MEANING OF PURPOSE

Like genius, purpose goes by many names and descriptions, and many wise contemporary thinkers have explored it. Laurence Boldt called it a "mission" and asked, "What is the message you want your life to proclaim?"[2] Deepak Chopra suggested that we ask ourselves how we are best suited to serve humanity.[3] James Redfield called it "the mission only we can do."[4] Contemporary psychotherapist Thomas Moore wrote of it as a vocation, "a calling from a place that is the source of meaning and identity."[5] Matthew Fox also wrote of purpose as a vocation, a call to participate in the work of the universe, and referred to it as a "cosmic role."[6] Richard Leider refers to purpose as "Your aim. Your reason for being. Your reason for getting up in the morning."[7]

Those of us who wrestle with understanding purpose, despite the disparity of our language, seem to agree on at least these four lines of reasoning:

1. Your purpose is not to be invented. It is, rather, to be discovered or detected. Redfield writes, "We all have a spiritual purpose, a mission, that we have been pursuing without being fully aware of it, and once we bring it completely into consciousness, our lives can take off."[8] Stephen Covey states, "I think each of us has an internal monitor or sense, a conscience, that gives us an awareness of our own uniqueness and the singular contributions that we can make."[9] Leider writes, "Purpose is already within us. It is waiting to be discovered."[10] And Rick Warren states that recognition of our purpose arrives not through looking within but through revelation.[11]

This point of agreement suggests that you should avoid trying to create a picture of what you think your purpose should be. Your purpose is a calling; thus, detecting it is an act of observing rather than inventing.

2. Your purpose is directed outward. Your purpose is a specific external expression of your genius. It infuses your activities in the world and is not solely within yourself or for yourself. Your genius is your gift to the world, and your purpose is a specific, unique, and tangible way in which the gift is given.

Viktor Frankl, who might be considered the grandfather of modern thinking about life purpose, said it in this way:

> One should not search for an abstract meaning of life. Everyone has his own specific vocation or mission in life to carry out a concrete assignment, which demands fulfillment. Therein he cannot be replaced, nor can his life be repeated. Thus, everyone's task is as unique as is his specific opportunity to implement it.[12]

Tom, who calls his genius Finding Jewels, owns and manages a business that buys and rents out homes and apartments. Tom sees his purpose as providing good housing at reasonable cost. The jewels he finds are attractive, well-priced homes and apartments and the people who rent from him.

Alan, a former marketing executive who now leads an executive placement company, says that his purpose is to create organizations composed solely of people doing their right work. Toni, who counsels people through transitions, says that her purpose is helping others identify their truths and serving the poor in spirit. Marlon, a training manager for a large corporation, describes his purpose as actualizing the potential of others. And Maya, a massage therapist, made a unique connection between her genius and her purpose. Maya calls her genius Remembering Spirit. She believes that her work involves helping people connect the energy of their spirits with their bodies and says that her purpose is "remembering" spirit, a play on the words she uses to describe her genius.

You do not pursue your purpose because it is self-satisfying, nor because it is rewarding in the conventional terms of power, prestige, fame, happiness, or wealth. You pursue it because you must. Purpose may also be thought of as a divine compulsion.

3. If you know your purpose, you can be more intentional and effective in fulfilling it. Williamson writes: "We are to do what there is a deep psychological and emotional imperative for us to do. That's our point of power, the source of our brilliance."[13]

Neil, whose genius is Exploring Pathways, works as a travel planner in addition to other creative endeavors. His agency prides itself on helping people find adventures and explorations that will be satisfying and unique. He thoroughly enjoys exploring pathways with his clients. "What is the best path for this person?" he asks himself when he is trying to help a client make a decision. He speaks of his purpose as providing both adventure and peace.

4. Purpose gives focus to a life. Purpose directs your decisions about what to do, when to do it, where to live, with whom to associate, and what to turn away from. Leider calls it "the quality we shape our lives around."[14]

SEEING A NEED

Philosopher Sam Keen wrote of a spiritual calling that involves four elements: a gift, a delight, a need, and a discipline.[15] The gift is your genius. The delight is your genius at work in a way that brings you joy. The need that only you can fulfill helps you identify your purpose. And the discipline is developing yourself in whatever ways are required in order to bring your genius to fulfill your purpose.

The story of Michael Azzopardi presents a rich opportunity to investigate this concept of purpose. It also illustrates that purpose has a seed, a precursor. Perceiving a need is not quite enough. Purpose is truly revealed in a compelling insight about what is required to fulfill the need.

The fruit of Azzopardi's purpose lies along the road between the villages of Siggiewi and Ghar Lapsi, on the island of Malta. It is Id-Dar tal-Providenza—The House of Divine Providence—a home for mentally and physically challenged people that was conceived and created by Azzopardi.

During the early 1920s, the young Azzopardi studied law at Malta University but switched to theology when it became clear to him that he was destined for the priesthood. Later in that decade, he was given the opportunity to study at the Gregorian Institute in Rome. He viewed this opportunity as a great honor, was thrilled to have it bestowed on him, and dreamed of the prestigious assignment that seemed sure to come his way after graduation. He thought he was fated for greatness and a life of prestige and service. He was, but in no way that he could have imagined.

Azzopardi was surprised and deeply disappointed when, after his studies in Rome were completed, he was ordered back to Malta in the role of a humble priest. But he did not allow his dreams to die, deciding that if he were ever to get the prestigious assignment he believed was surely his, he would have to be the best priest the Catholic Church had ever seen.

Years passed. He taught religion in a secondary school and led retreats for teenagers. He acted as a chaplain during World War II. He chaired a committee to oversee the creation of a center of Catholic culture in Malta. He traveled the countryside visiting the sick and the elderly. He went on the radio with weekly broadcasts for those unable to attend Mass and with a show explaining each Sunday's gospel.

He also made surprising and disturbing discoveries. He saw a need.

Azzopardi discovered mentally and physically challenged children hidden away by their families. He learned of children whose existence was unknown to neighbors, locked away during the day as their families worked in the fields or otherwise made a living. These children touched him deeply, as did the families who hid them and whose shame about them was profound. He began to conceive of a home for the children, many of whom came from impoverished families.

A COMPELLING INSIGHT

The insight that fuels purpose arrives when we see what is and then look beyond it or see it in a new way. This insight reaches further than the mere perception of a need; it advocates a way to fulfill the need. Azzopardi had found such an insight, the seed of his specific and concrete purpose: the children would be given a nurturing and accepting environment, the families would receive assistance, and the community would have the opportunity to rid itself of the shame it harbored.

On September 12, 1965, Azzopardi spoke of his idea during his weekly radio broadcast. When he returned to his home, a woman stood outside the door, clutching an envelope. She had been waiting there for him for more than four hours.

He approached her, and she told him that she had heard his radio appeal for a home for handicapped children. She offered the envelope to him, explaining that it contained money she had been saving for a vacation. She was giving the money to him instead, to start, she said, "your home for the children."

Azzopardi later described this moment as a significant turning point in his life. I heard him say, "I knew that if I took that envelope, my life would never be what I had expected it to be and would never be the same as it had been." Until that moment, he had not thought of the home as his but simply considered it a good idea. A good idea is, without doubt, not the same as a compelling insight. I feel certain that you, like me and everyone else, have many good ideas that you never act on. They may be good ideas, but they do not compel us to act.

Azzopardi hesitated for an instant, deciding whether to commit himself, to allow himself to be compelled. And then he took the envelope. It contained 100 Maltese pounds, about $300. He had been a parish priest for thirty years. He was fifty-five years old.

Today, Id-Dar tal-Providenza consists of three villas, each housing a different age group of physically and mentally challenged children and adults, and is noted as one of the best homes of its kind in Europe. Azzopardi, with obvious pride, described the home.

> Beautiful airy rooms, recreation areas, chapels, gardens, shops and classrooms, kitchens, dining rooms, laundry rooms, a physiotherapy center properly equipped, and a large and beautiful gymnasium; an occupational therapy department including a pottery unit; a spacious Social hall for Staff meetings, reunions of parents, benefactors and friends, for film shows and theatricals as well as for music therapy and anything else that helps to keep these beloved "angels" happy and contented.[16]

Azzopardi died in 1987, having devoted his last twenty-two years to those he fondly called his "angels," the physically and mentally challenged residents of Id-Dar tal-Providenza. Many Maltese people think of him as a saint. His good friend Lewis Portelli wrote about Azzopardi just after his death:

> Perhaps one of his greatest achievements . . . was his herculean feat in persuading parents and relatives to "take out" their handicapped, many times from the "hidden" places where they were kept. He was the one who convinced everyone that having a sick or handicapped member in the family was nothing to be ashamed of.[17]

GENIUS AND PURPOSE

My one meeting with Azzopardi was brief, and I cannot say how he would have described his genius. Portelli wrote that he was "always looking ahead and beyond."[18] He was a visionary who saw what was and imagined what was possible. He also looked beyond the rough surface of agrarian life to see beauty and wonder. He looked beyond the children's handicaps and saw them as "angels." He looked beyond the shame of their families and saw people in distress. He looked beyond whatever Id-Dar tal-Providenza was at any particular time and saw what it could and should become. The first residents were children, but children would become adolescents, who would need a different kind of place, and adolescents would become adults. He saw all of this, and so Id-Dar tal-Providenza has three villas, one for children, one for adolescents, and one for adults. When Azzopardi was studying in Rome, he looked beyond that period toward a new assignment. And when he was assigned to be a parish priest on Malta, he immediately began looking beyond that as well.

Was Azzopardi's genius Looking Beyond? I suspect it was that, or something quite similar. He might have used different words. But even if his exact words cannot be known, it is known that Azzopardi's gift—his genius—was firmly directed toward what Keen termed a "spiritual calling" and which I refer to as "purpose." Azzopardi saw a need, and, beyond that, he found a compelling insight. Through his life experiences up to the moment in 1965 when the woman presented him with her envelope, he had developed the discipline he needed to fulfill the purpose he was offered.

WHERE TO LOOK FOR CLUES

Most calls are not as vivid or as direct as Azzopardi's. We must make ourselves available to compelling insights, never knowing when or where they will arise, or even how to make them arise. The source of insight is intuition, a particularly elusive quality and one not amenable to the promptings of planning, analysis, or even rational thought.

But even though we cannot produce compelling insights at will, we can learn to listen for the small voice that announces them and to recognize whatever envelope is handed to us. We could also turn our attention to those experiences within which insight and purpose reveal themselves. It appears that there are at least seven such places. Much like the fields of experience you explored while recognizing your genius, they bear exploration because they might contain important clues:

- Strong emotions

- What other people ask of you

- Unexpected experiences and turning points

- Your suffering

- Meditation and prayer

- Family history

- Recurring ideas

Strong Emotions

Azzopardi took the envelope that was handed to him partly because he had long experienced strong feelings about the challenged and neglected children of Malta and their families. The trick to detecting purpose through strong emotions is to avoid or minimize feelings of victimization caused by the inevitable negative events that often provoke them and to move toward creative action.

Use **Exercise 18** to explore strong emotions for clues to your purpose (see page 150).

What Other People Ask of You

Toni was divorced at the age of forty-two, after twenty years of marriage. It was a traumatic event for her. She says, "I was absolutely programmed to be a wife and mother. And nice Catholic girls from Baton Rouge just don't get divorced."

Toni sought help from a counseling service that specialized in helping people who were experiencing troubling transitions like divorce and the death of a loved one. During counseling, she was led to question her programming and seek her own truth. She recalls, "I literally had to ask myself questions like, 'What color do I like, really?' and 'What music do I like, really?'"

After she had passed through this difficult transition, the people who ran the agency, recognizing her strength, skill, determination, and capacity for empathy, asked her to volunteer as a counselor. Metaphorically speaking, they, like the woman who had waited

Use **Exercise 19** to find clues to your purpose by exploring what others ask of you (see page 151).

outside Azzopardi's door, handed her an envelope. Fifteen years later, she is quite successful in her own business of counseling people in transition and leading workshops. She is fulfilling her purpose: helping others identify their truth and serving the poor in spirit.

Unexpected Experiences and Turning Points

Toni did not expect to get divorced, and the divorce itself was a significant turning point. Alan experienced something similar. He was fired. He engaged in some deep soul-searching after he was fired, and this experience became a major turning point in his life.

"Actually," he says, "I fired myself. In truth, I made it impossible for my employer to keep me. It was the wrong work for me."

Use **Exercise 20** to explore unexpected experiences and turning points for clues to your purpose (see page 152).

During his soul-searching, he thought about his work history and read and talked with experts about the nature of work. This led to his current career heading an executive placement firm. He had found his purpose: to create organizations composed solely of people doing their right work.

Unexpected experiences do not automatically become turning points. Azzopardi could have declined the envelope. Toni could have said "no" to the request that she become a volunteer counselor. Alan might have felt victimized, blamed his boss, and gone on to another job failure.

Your Suffering

Viktor Frankl's system of Logotherapy grew out of his suffering in a Nazi concentration camp. Frankl believed that suffering could be a source of meaning in life if we alter our attitude toward it. He writes:

> We must never forget that we may also find meaning in life even when confronted with a hopeless situation, when facing a fate that cannot be changed. For what then matters is to bear witness to the uniquely human potential at its best, which is to transform a personal

tragedy into a triumph, to turn one's predicament into a human achievement.[19]

Maya, for example, is a victim of childhood abuse. She also recalls that, as a child, she knew deep inside herself that there is more to life than what she saw around her. She remembers carrying that sense throughout her life, even when she was most afraid. As a massage therapist, she helps people connect their bodies and spirits and respect their physical selves.

Use **Exercise 21** to explore your suffering for clues to your purpose (see page 155).

It is easy to adopt a victimlike attitude toward suffering. Maya did, for many years. It was only after much self-exploration, aided from time to time by therapists and support groups, that she was able to transform her attitude toward her childhood suffering.

She says, "Having the courage to be a survivor and knowing that my life is more than what happens on the surface are the two major things that formed my purpose."

As with negative emotions, detecting a purpose in suffering requires that we avoid or minimize feeling victimized and move into creative action.

Meditation and Prayer

Rick Warren writes that the struggle we experience when trying to uncover purpose results in part from speculation—guessing and theorizing about our purpose. He proposes an alternative to speculation: revelation. Warren seeks revelation in his Christian faith.

Use **Exercise 22** to explore meditation and prayer for clues to your purpose (see page 156).

Rabbi Zalman Schachter-Shalomi found the revelation that set a course for his later years during a self-directed forty-day retreat taken as he neared the age of sixty. He came away from the retreat with a "vision of elderhood" that eventually became the Spiritual Eldering Institute, which describes itself as a multifaith organization dedicated to the spiritual dimensions of aging and conscious living.[20]

After Alan was fired, he took to walking the banks of a nearby river. He did this every day for nearly six months. He said, "In order to detect my purpose, I had to calm down and quiet my mind, so that I could hear the small voice inside me that knew what I was supposed to do next. Walking the river, throwing sticks into the water, and watching them float away was a form of meditation."

Although your purpose is to be detected from the many messages around you, some form of meditation—quieting the mind—can be immensely valuable. Revelation rarely, if ever, visits a turbulent mind. Azzopardi's purpose was handed to him. For most of us, however, the call is not so blatant or dramatic. We must listen carefully.

Family History

Several years ago, my sister and I took our septuagenarian mother to lunch on Mother's Day. In the middle of lunch, and seemingly out of nowhere, my mother asked me, "Do you ever paint?" I had not painted in nearly twenty-five years and was surprised that she thought I might.

"I always hoped you would follow in your grandfather's and uncle's footsteps," she said sadly.

My grandfather, after retiring from the U.S. Postal Service, created vivid oil paintings of sailing ships and harbors and western scenes imagined from Zane Grey novels. My uncle, for whom I was named, was a graphic artist. I took a circuitous route from high school to college, spending four intervening years as an apprentice to him and studying advertising design in the evenings at an art school. During those years, I discovered I was more interested in people than in paint. I left my job, entered college to study psychology, and put my art supplies away, pretty much for good.

It would seem, on the surface, that my mother's aspirations to raise a painter went unfulfilled. Still, there is a clue here about my purpose. As I was writing my first book, *Artful Work,* I found myself reaching back to my own past, to my art training. The book is a synthesis of my experience as an artist and as a management consultant, an attempt to integrate artistry with work. My experience as a practicing artist became the grounding for guiding others to find the artistry in their own work.

Likewise, Maya sees her history of childhood abuse as grounding for her purpose.

Use **Exercise 23** to explore your family history for clues to your purpose (see page 157).

Redfield proposes another way of searching our family history for clues about our own purpose. He writes that purpose is a spiritual path involving the discovery of a truth that synthesizes your parents' beliefs. Redfield's protagonist is searching for a sacred manuscript. In the course of his journey, he meets a priest, Father Carl, who tells him,

> We are not merely the physical creation of our parents; we are also the spiritual creation. . . . To discover your real self, you must admit that the real you began in a position between their truths. That's why you were born there; to take a higher perspective on what they stood for.[21]

Redfield's protagonist reflects that his father's life was about maximizing his aliveness, while his mother's was about sacrifice and service. The question for him becomes how to live a life that includes both. Father Carl tells him to look closely at what has happened to him since birth. He says, "If you view your life as one story, from birth to right now, you'll be able to see how you have been working on this question all along."[22]

Recurring Ideas

Toni is interested in alternative living arrangements for senior citizens. She once visited a monastery for a weekend retreat. When she told friends about her experience, many expressed a desire for a similar experience, but not in a religious context.

Use **Exercise 24** to explore recurring ideas for clues to your purpose (see page 158).

Toni's recurring idea is to create a worldwide network of group housing arrangements for senior citizens that would also serve as retreat centers. The senior citizens would manage and staff the centers. This idea has recurred frequently. It is provoked by many things, such as brochures arriving in the mail announcing retreats and visits to an elderly aunt who lives alone. The idea has haunted Toni over many years, and she now believes she must act on it in some way.

For many years, Alan has thought of writing a book. He knows the theme and has the book outlined. This recurring idea has become a stronger presence, and he is about to take a sabbatical from his job in order to write.

GETTING IT

Use **Exercises 25 and 26** to explore potential additional clues to your purpose (see pages 159 and 160).

As you search for your purpose, the question in your mind is the same as the one you asked about genius: How will I know when I have gotten it right? And the answer is the same: When you have gotten it right, you will know it is right. You will experience an Aha! and a felt sense of rightness.

You will also see that your purpose is a vehicle for expressing your genius and that the life you have lived until the moment it reveals itself has been preparation for its coming.

Tune Your Self

Not everything that is faced can be changed,
but nothing can be changed until it is faced.

—JAMES BALDWIN

THE BIBLICAL PARABLE of the talents tells of a man who was preparing for a journey and brought three servants together before his departure. He dispensed to each of them large sums of money called "talents." He gave five talents to one servant, two to another, and one to the third, apportioning them in relation to each servant's abilities. The servant who received five talents used them to trade and doubled his talents. The servant who received three talents likewise doubled his. The servant who received one talent hid it by burying it in the ground. The master returned home. On discovering that the first and second servants had doubled their talents, he rewarded them by appointing them to positions of authority; each was placed "in charge of many things." On discovering that the third servant had buried his single talent, the man took it away from him, berated him for being "wicked and lazy," and cast him out of the house and "into the outer darkness."[1]

Biblical scholars draw many lessons from the parable of the talents, including lessons about our responsibility for that which has been bestowed upon us. It is not a mere play on words to insist that you risk peril if you do not take responsibility for the talents

Use **Exercise 27** to examine tendencies that facilitate or hinder you in bringing your genius to your purpose (see page 162).

that have been entrusted to you. Your genius and purpose are talents in the sense described in the parable. They are treasures entrusted to you by whatever Higher Authority you acknowledge, to use in whatever community you embrace, for the benefit of the Higher Authority, the community, and yourself.

This is a threefold responsibility. One responsibility is to recognize and nurture your genius. Another is to detect and act on your purpose. The third is to tune your self as the instrument that focuses your genius outward and in unswerving support of your purpose.

I am using the term *self* as a catch-all word to include the sum of everything you have learned about who you are, how the world works, and your place in the world. I might instead have used terms such as *personality* or *makeup*. Think of your self as the psychological aspect of your being as distinct from the spiritual aspect that is your soul and genius. This self was the decisive difference between the two servants who made fruitful use of what had been given to them and the third servant, who did not.

The self can be viewed as a covering—a kind of skin, shell, or crust—that forms around your soul and genius as you experience the world. That covering facilitates the process of bringing the energy of your genius to your purpose. For example, if you learn optimism, you are more likely to succeed. But the covering can also interfere in troublesome ways. The tendencies to procrastinate, to believe you are not good enough or educated enough, to fear failure or success, to fail to nurture yourself or find nurturing others—all of these tendencies and many others throw you off course and perhaps even into a deep ditch.

The diagram on the opposite page, from Chapter 1, shows your self as a straight arrow, a channel directing the energy of your genius head-on at your purpose. It often does not work that way, but this is an ideal to which to aspire.

So there is yet another element of complexity involved in bringing your genius to work. It isn't enough to recognize your genius and detect your purpose. There is also all of that muddled

Life and Work

Genius   *SELF*   Purpose

stuff in the middle, matters about which people such as psychiatrists, psychologists, philosophers, counselors, educators, clergymen, theologians, and sages have talked, written, and argued for centuries.

FINDING YOUR OWN ANSWERS

How to bring it all together? How to align your genius, your purpose, your self, and your work, all the while conducting your life in a complex world during turbulent times that now and again seem to want to swallow you whole? There is no answer that fits every person. There is only a challenge that every person must accept.

Rainer Maria Rilke told a young poet:

> I would like to beg you, dear Sir, as well as I can, to have patience with everything unresolved in your heart and to try to love the questions themselves as if they were locked rooms or books written in a very foreign language.[2]

I have posed four questions in this book. They have proved to be fruitful for many people, as individual questions and as a set. First, What is your genius? Second, Is your genius at work? Third, What is your purpose? And fourth, Is your genius on purpose? If you do not yet have answers to these questions, heed Rilke's advice: love the questions. Tumble them gently over and over in your mind but recognize that the answers lie closer to the heart and spirit. Acknowledge that the answers sometimes come easily but may also be hard to gain, that they may be surprising, and that they may not arrive at the moment when you believe you need them.

In this closing chapter, I will tell a few more stories. They are about genius and purpose, self, life, and work, and about people who, at least for a time, did meld these aspects of their lives in answer to the four key questions. I am offering them as examples of how some people have lived the questions and have found their own answers. And while it would be impossible to adequately explore the complex and intricate role of self in this or any other single book, I do want to illuminate three aspects of self that are crucial to bringing it all together: responsibility, awareness, and courage. When you develop these three qualities, you will create a platform, as shown in the diagram below, upon which your genius, self, and purpose can come fully alive.

A BREWING SENSE OF PURPOSE

Vanessa earned an undergraduate degree in management information systems and went to work for a large company. She found that it was not what she wanted to do. Managers would tell her what needed to be developed, and she often thought, and sometimes said, "Why would we do that? Why don't we do it this way?" She was dismayed and perplexed until somebody said to

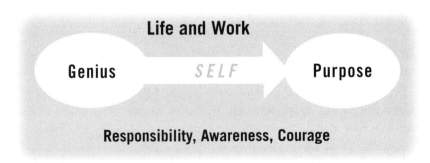

Life and Work

Genius *SELF* **Purpose**

Responsibility, Awareness, Courage

her, "I really think you need to be a business analyst and not a developer." That comment opened her eyes to the possibility of altering the focus of her career.

Vanessa was able to reshape her work so that she helped the technical people in the organization communicate with their nontechnical counterparts, and she loved it. Consequently, she began leading projects and eventually started her own business. She and her husband have two young sons, and she thought that running her own business would give her more control over her time.

She said, "So there I was, a contract project manager, which I wouldn't wish on anybody."

Vanessa then came to a realization that had been brewing for some time. She described it this way: "The technical group was missing the concept of how people change. They didn't know how to break down the organizational barriers they were running into."

That realization led to another career move. "I abandoned my own business and went to work for someone again so that I could figure out how to bring the human side into technical projects."

After earning her undergraduate degree, working at three successive jobs, and starting her own business, Vanessa had detected the purpose of her work: to bring human concerns into technical work.

RESPONSIBILITY

So far, Vanessa's story describes her search for purpose. Within it also lies a significant subtext—the theme of responsibility. You are responsible for who you are and can become, for your genius and purpose, and for managing the sometimes meddlesome self. This involves acting in accordance with a considered view about how you must be in the world. It demands an understanding of how your perception creates your reality as well as the ability to make good judgments about how you helped construct the circumstances that surround you. It requires willingness to see yourself as the author of your self, to understand and accept that you are the creator of your own feelings, thoughts, beliefs, perceptions, and actions.

Responsibility is the antithesis of blame, which is a difficult issue in our society. We most often want to know who is at fault. If we stop blaming others, luck, or fate yet hold on to the need for blame, we will blame ourselves. Responsibility requires that we let go of the idea of blame altogether.

When you assume a responsible orientation, you do not blame others, luck, or fate for what you are being, doing, having, or feeling; you avoid blaming yourself; you are aware of your contribution to your own life and of the multitude of choices you have in any given situation; and you tune your self to become the precise instrument of your genius and purpose. You ask instead, "What has happened, what is the situation, how did I contribute, what is to be learned, and what shall I do next?" Letting go of the idea of blame does not mean that certain deeds should go unpunished. It means that if you wish to adopt a responsible orientation to your life, you must move away from the victim orientation that is the source of blame.

When you assume this responsibility, you set yourself free of the curse of victimization. You may be victimized, to be sure, but you will refuse to think, feel, and act like a victim. Viktor Frankl wrote, "When we are no longer able to change a situation—just think of an incurable disease such as inoperable cancer—we are challenged to change ourselves."[3]

Most of us feel victimized even in situations that we had a hand in creating. We visit mean and cranky Uncle Charley because we feel sorry for him, but we wish we were somewhere else. We write a report for a boss, although we know no one will ever read it and we would rather be doing something else. We spend a frustrating hour waiting in an empty parking lot for an auto mechanic to arrive to jump-start our car. We would rather be anywhere else.

In circumstances like these, we feel that time is being stolen from us, that our moments are not our own. But this feeling is illusory. The moments are ours even if we have chosen to use them in ways that are less than satisfying. We are the ones, after all, who decide to visit Uncle Charley, write the report, or wait in the parking lot. We always have an alternative. We can hold on to our sense of responsibility by acknowledging our own decisions.

I do not mean to imply that we should never go and visit Uncle Charley. I do mean that we should go, if we choose to go, with full knowledge that we are there because we chose to be. If we hate the experience, let's not blame Uncle Charley for that, even if he does get cranky. I am using Uncle Charley as a stand-in for everyone in your life who seems to require something from you that you are ambivalent about giving.

Often, we do such things in order to avoid something far more uncomfortable. For example, putting up with Uncle Charley's crankiness means we don't have to feel guilty about not going to see him. So let us just admit that we are visiting Uncle Charley knowing that he will probably be unpleasant and we accept the unpleasantness as a fair exchange for guilt. Fine. At least we come away with a clear sense of our own participation in the event. We are being honest with ourselves and are taking responsibility for ourselves.

When we lay blame, whatever we blame seems somehow to get bigger than it actually is. Uncle Charley becomes the size of Godzilla. The object of blame occupies a larger space in our minds. We think about it a lot. We talk about it a lot. It takes up psychic and emotional space that could probably be put to better use.

Of course, bigger is relative. When we use psychic and emotional space in this way, what really gets bigger is our sense of being victimized. What gets smaller is our sense of our own responsibility. Your impulses to blame others, luck, or fate are early warning signals that you are about to cede responsibility.

Blame is usually the result of an internal conflict that we would rather avoid. If we don't visit Uncle Charley, we will feel guilty. But if we do visit him, we will feel resentful. The conflict has everything to do with us and not much to do with Uncle Charley. The alternatives are to either give up feeling guilty for not visiting or to give up feeling resentful when we do visit. But the seeds of such guilt and resentment lie buried in the psyche, and we may have to do some digging around in aspects of our selves that we would rather leave alone. So, in attempting to avoid those seeds, we blame Uncle Charley, and in so doing, we avoid our own responsibility.

Use **Exercise 28** to examine the internal conflicts that produce blame (see page 163).

When Vanessa felt dismayed that her training in systems development had led her to unsatisfying work, she reshaped her job. When she came to the insight that there was little understanding within the technical community about how people change, she left her own business to work in a place where she could explore the problem. When she was not able to change a situation, she met the challenge to change herself. When you operate from a position of responsibility, problems become the seeds of opportunity.

A friend tells the sad story of an acquaintance, a fiftyish mid-level executive in a large company. When he was an up-and-coming young manager, he had what he thought was a brilliant but time-sensitive idea. He was scheduled to make a trip with a very senior executive, knew they would be sitting together, and eagerly awaited the opportunity to pitch the idea. On board the plane, however, he found that another man was seated between him and the senior executive. He never did pitch the idea. Although he now has a fifteenth-floor office, he believes that had he not been the victim of an unlucky seat assignment, he would surely have reached the higher floors. Taking responsibility for your genius and purpose, and for tuning yourself, will help you avoid becoming that man.

A SOLID FELT SENSE

Vanessa returned to her own business. She had been seeking a name for her genius for more than a year. At one point, she thought she had discovered the right name—Making Connections—but it didn't wear well over time. There was something more to her genius, but she could not grasp what was missing.

While she was discussing her genius with a colleague, she thought of the name Illuminating the Heart. She said to her colleague, "It isn't like I'm actually making a connection. It's more like I'm bringing light to a connection. And it isn't just the connection that's important. It's also the heart: sometimes people's hearts, sometimes the heart of an issue, and sometimes the heart of a group's problem."

This name felt so right to her at the time that she bought a bracelet to commemorate its discovery. But weeks later, something nagged at the edge of her consciousness. The name wasn't quite right, but her inability to find the right name did not disturb her.

"My genius is more at work in my life and work than it ever has been—even though I can't pinpoint it," she said. "Sometimes I feel pressure to find a name because I think it will help me solidify, but most days I don't. I do know it has given me incredible confidence. And I absolutely know that my genius is at work even though I can't name it. I still wear the bracelet when I am with other people—it means everything to me."

Vanessa had, if not the right name for her genius, the more important felt sense of it. And, she said, "I know what I do has value."

AWARENESS

Awareness is another aspect of self that contributes to the platform on which your genius, self, and purpose come alive. When well developed and finely tuned, awareness stretches in many directions. It attends to your physical, intellectual, emotional, and spiritual well-being. It takes care of the circumstances of your life: the people with whom you engage, the activities in which you participate, and your living and working environments. It alerts you to those aspects of your self, your life, and your work that nourish and support your genius and purpose and those that do not.

Vanessa's finely tuned awareness alerted her to her dissatisfaction with her first job, then to her desire to construct a life that allowed her more control over her time, and then to the need to put her own business aside for a while as she pursued her purpose

Use **Exercise 29** to begin improving your awareness (see page 164).

in a different way. It helped her to see that the name Making Connections did not fully explain her genius because it did not explain her deep need to bring light to connections.

Jayson, whose genius is Maximizing Opportunities, provides insight about the ways in which taking responsibility for your genius and purpose in itself enhances your awareness. He has worked at many things but considers himself first and foremost a teacher.

He said, "Knowing my genius makes it apparent why I pursue certain things. I pursue things because I see potential in them, and I feel frustrated when potential is not realized. But I don't try to pursue every possibility, because if I did, I couldn't maximize any of them. Knowing my genius explains a whole lot of things to me, such as my successes, how I approach things, my relationships, and problems."

Jayson also described how knowledge of his genius increased his awareness in his role as a parent. "When I look at other people —people I work with, my wife, my children—and I see the things that are possible, and then I see lack of effort, it's the most frustrating thing in the world to me. One of my daughters is a B student. She doesn't study. I tell her, 'You could be getting into any college you want and you're watching cartoons?' But that's about me, and I can let go of some of it. It's at least helpful to know that my frustration is contributing to my understanding of myself—maximizing my possibilities for growth, if not hers."

Dan, whose genius is Charting the Course, related a similar tale of the frustration he experiences whenever he attempts to chart the course of his teenage son's life. Tales such as these are good reminders that our gifts are not always welcomed by others.

Entering into the challenge of recognizing your genius stretches your awareness in two ways. First, it helps you connect the seemingly unconnected things that you do. For example, Jayson is an avid golfer. He said, "I didn't take up golf until I was thirty, and now I'm a range rat and close to scratch. I found that the opportunity to be a good golfer exists within me, and I want to maximize it."

He has also given musical instruments—a guitar, banjo, dulcimer, and mandolin—to his brother, who is musically gifted. Jayson is able to connect the dots between his attempts to influence his daughter, his golfing hobby, his gifts to his brother, and his primary vocation, teaching. All are about maximizing potential. Making the connection provides him with a solid sense of identity and wholeness, a sense of "This is who I am."

When you acknowledge your genius and purpose as divinely inspired, you also gain connection to the spiritual aspect of your life and increase awareness in that realm as well. As Tia said, "I know my genius has been with me always. I believe it is undeniably and unavoidably the energy of my soul."

So while a modicum of awareness is needed to begin building the platform on which genius, self, and purpose come alive, that awareness will continue to grow as you engage in the process itself.

COURAGE

Along with responsibility and awareness, you will also need the courage to act in ways that are consistent with your genius and purpose even when you cannot guess the future, when fears about personal inadequacy, success, or failure rear up threateningly, or when your very identity seems in doubt. In this regard, I have one more story to tell.

Use **Exercise 30** to determine who supports your genius and purpose (see page 165).

Jocylin was close to her father when she was a small child. He was a stonemason and loved to show her his work. He also let her work with him on small projects around their home. At the age of six, Jocylin knew how to point bricks and was beginning to understand what it meant to build things.

By the time Jocylin was in high school, her father was running a contracting business, and she often visited his office while he prepared estimates, ordered material, and spoke with customers and architects. She enjoyed the atmosphere in the office and began to help out after school and during weekends. When she finished high school, she knew what she wanted to do with her life: first, she wanted to work in her father's business, and then she wanted to run it.

Jocylin's father died during her senior year in high school, and her older brother took over the business. Jocylin told her brother of her wish to enter the family business.

"Eventually," she told him, "I would like to run the business."

He said, "No. Get married. Have children." Other family members agreed.

Jocylin did get married. She moved away from the town where she had grown up and had three children. Money was tight for her family, so she attended sewing classes and made most of the clothing for herself and her children and did alterations for her husband and for friends. She began to understand creating clothing as she had once understood building with brick—the two were somehow similar.

Jocylin still wanted to run a business. She inquired about earning a business degree. But money remained tight, and her husband was unsupportive.

Twenty-five years after her marriage, Jocylin's husband died. She said, "The day after my husband's funeral, I walked to the end of the road that passes in front of my home and asked, 'Now what?'" She had no college degree, no credentials of any kind, two teenagers still in high school, and little money. She was forty-three years old. Fears about inadequacy enveloped her. She thought with dread of the woman who had come to scrub the floors of her parents' house.

Standing there, facing a barren piece of ground, she asked herself, "What do I know about?" The answer was, clothing.

Putting aside her fears about her lack of a business education, Jocylin started a small boutique, which grew into a larger boutique, which became an even larger boutique. She owned not only the business but also the building that housed it and two apartments. Jocylin became a successful businesswoman.

When asked about her purpose, she said, "I loved my father's business because he helped people get what they wanted in a creative way, and in a way they could afford. 'You want a brick wall? Here's a creative brick wall at a fair price.' I do the same thing. 'You want clothing? Here's creative clothing at a fair price. It's different from the clothing worn by the person who lives next door to you.' The clothing I sell isn't found in the mall, and people can afford it."

Jocylin calls her genius Forming the True. The words are rich in meaning for her. The word *forming* suggests the forms stonemasons use for constructing foundations and those tailors use to shape clothing. The word *true* means something like "natural" to her. Bricks are composed of natural elements, and her shop specializes in garments made of natural fibers such as cotton, wool, and silk. She tries to help customers find clothing that will make them feel true to themselves. And she views her life as one long voyage toward forming her true self.

Use **Exercise 31** to examine your courage (see page 166).

About her decision to open a boutique, Jocylin said, "I was afraid. But because I was afraid, I knew it was the thing I had to do."

Courage does not mean the absence of fear. It means, rather, acting in spite of fear or because fear is a clue that something that will challenge you is dawning. I once heard a man described derisively as a person who "thinks an insight is a real change." The comment suggests that an insight may produce a change within the person who has it, but it only becomes a meaningful change when the person does something because of it that produces a difference that extends beyond the self. Courage is doing.

There are many examples of courage in these pages. Jocylin started a business despite her fears. Michael Azzopardi accepted the envelope that was offered to him and began a new life at the age of fifty-five. Maya faced down childhood abuse to become a successful massage therapist and fulfill her purpose, of "remembering" spirit. Francine left a relatively secure, high-paying job in order to bring her genius—Engaging the Heart—to her work. Vanessa took the risk of asking her boss to restructure her job. Alicia doggedly sought her genius for five years. Neil held on to his genius—Exploring Pathways—despite the negative labels that were assigned to him.

Use **Exercise 32** to summarize what you have learned about your genius, purpose, and self, and to plan your next steps (see page 168).

Many fears reflect real danger and must be respected. But many reflect a state of mind—I can't, I shouldn't, I'm wrong, I'm somehow not enough. This kind of fear must be challenged in order to bring your genius, self, and purpose alive. Then, in the words of a most courageous person, Eleanor Roosevelt, "You gain strength, courage and confidence by every experience in which you really stop to look fear in the face. You must do the thing which you think you cannot do."[4]

It is my hope that you will come to recognize your genius, detect your purpose, tune your self, and do the things you must do. And whenever you ask, "Is my genius at work and on purpose?" I hope your answer will be "Yes!"

Exercises for Answering the Four Key Questions

THE FOLLOWING EXERCISES ARE DESIGNED to help you find answers to the four key questions posed in this book. Each of the exercises has proved to be helpful to some people, but no single exercise is helpful to everyone. Do not expect that any one exercise will provide you with all of the information you need. The process for recognizing your genius and that for detecting your purpose will be as unique to you as are your genius and purpose themselves. Both processes usually require an accumulation of information from several exercises and life experiences before you reach a critical mass of information and the right name for your genius emerges or your purpose becomes apparent. If a particular exercise does not seem helpful to you, go on to a different one.

It is sometimes useful to revisit exercises that you have already completed. The subconscious often continues working on questions even when we are not consciously engaged with them. When you revisit an exercise, it may take on new meaning.

The exercises are organized according to the four questions. An additional exercise at the end is to be used to summarize your learning.

What is your genius? Exercises 1–13 will help you recognize your genius and reach your own understanding of the meaning of the concept. Most of the exercises are intended to help you generate words that might describe your genius. At the end of these exercises, you will be asked to test the resulting words to see if they do indeed describe your genius. You will be asked repeatedly to test these words because I cannot predict which exercise, if any, will lead directly to the right name for your genius.

Is your genius at work? Use Exercises 14–17 after you have come to recognize your genius. They will help you discover which aspects of your current work engage your genius and which aspects do not and explore what you can do to change the situation.

What is your purpose? Exercises 18–26 will help you examine the different fields of experience in which clues to your purpose might be found. As with the exercises that help you recognize your genius, I cannot predict which of these exercises, if any, will lead directly to understanding your purpose.

Is your genius on purpose? Use Exercises 27–31 after you have recognized your genius and detected your purpose. They will help you examine aspects of your self that facilitate or hinder bringing your genius and purpose to your work.

Summarize. Use Exercise 32 to help you summarize what you have learned.

EXERCISES

To answer the question "What is your genius?"

To answer the question "Is your genius at work?"

To answer the question "What is your purpose?"

To answer the question "Is your genius on purpose?"

Summarize

TO ANSWER THE QUESTION

"What Is Your Genius?"

Generating Words

One of the strategies for recognizing your genius involves generating lists of words—sometimes a lot of words—until they begin to form a pattern. The purpose of this four-step exercise is to help you generate words that might offer clues to your genius. The exercise is a starting point; words that come to mind first will probably be the most obvious ones. Then, as you continue with more exercises to generate still more words, patterns of words will begin to emerge.

You are looking for at least two words. The first one must be a gerund, a word that ends with *ing* and indicates action.

Step 1: List as many words as you can that end in *ing* and describe activities that you enjoy.

Step 2: List as many nouns as you can that describe what you naturally create around you. What do you "bring to the party"?

Step 3: Select one word from each of the two lists above that attracts you the most. Write the words in the boxes.

Choose a word from Step 1.

Choose a word from Step 2.

Step 4: Say it aloud. Using the two words that you chose in Step 3, say aloud, "My genius is _____ _____."

As you say the words, notice how you feel. Trust your felt sense of the rightness or wrongness of the words as a name for your genius.

Peeling the Onion

Recognizing your genius is much like peeling an onion. Imagine an onion in which the outer layers represent your skills, talents, behavior, accomplishments, interests, and creations. You have developed your talents and skills and produced your creations because they allowed your genius to express itself. Your interests, behavior, and accomplishments are also often expressions of your genius.

Step 1: Use the empty lines in the diagram below to make short lists of your skills, behavior, interests, talents, creations, and accomplishments.

Skills

_____

_____

_____

Behavior

_____

_____

_____

Interests

_____

_____

_____

Talents

_____

_____

_____

GENIUS

Creations

_____

_____

_____

Accomplishments

_____

_____

_____

EXERCISE 2 *(continued)*

Step 2: Look for a common denominator among the items that you listed. What goes into all or most of them? The common denominator should describe an activity that comes naturally to you.

Complete the sentence below by filling in the blanks (use a gerund in the first blank).

The common denominator among the items listed in Step 1 is . . .

_____ _____.

Noticing Yourself

Noticing is a three-step process for recognizing your genius. The first step is noticing what you do when you are not noticing what you do, the second is associating what you notice with other activities that seem similar, and the third is uncovering the common intent among the activities you noticed and the ones you associated with them.

Step 1: Notice what you do when you are not noticing what you do. For example, June noticed that she suggested creating a phone list of meeting participants even though no one had asked for such a list, and Dave noticed that he straightened up the meeting room.

Here is a list of things to begin noticing.

What is the first thing I think about when I enter a room?

_____

What is the first thing I do when I enter a room?

_____

What do I spontaneously contribute to the activity of a group?

_____

What kind of contribution do I often feel compelled to make to a discussion?

_____

What kinds of things do I feel compelled to do for others?

_____

What do I feel compelled to do simply because I enjoy it?

_____

Step 2: Associate what you notice with other activities that seem similar. Noticing by itself is not enough. Ask yourself, "What other activities do I engage in that seem similar?" For example, June suspected that her desire to create a phone list of meeting participants was somehow similar to collecting sewing patterns and planning a garden. Associate freely, without censoring yourself. Do not be concerned at this point with trying to understand how the activities are related to one another.

Note any of your activities that seem similar to those you listed in Step 1.

_____

_____

_____

Step 3: Uncover the common intent among the activities you noticed and the ones you associated with them. Your genius is an undercurrent of intention sweeping along beneath the surface of your activities. In order to uncover that undercurrent, ask yourself, "What do I intend to accomplish in all of the associated activities?" June said that her intent had something to do with creating a base from which to launch other activities. The phone list was a database. Her patterns were a base for sewing. Planning, preparing, and planting a garden created a base for growing flowers and vegetables. After making these associations and uncovering the common intent among them, she named her genius Building Platforms.

Complete the sentence below by filling in the blanks. For example, June filled the first blank with the word *building*, and the second with *platforms*. Use a gerund for the first word.

The common denominator among the items listed in Step 2 is . . .

_____   _____.

Step 4: Say it aloud. Using the two words that you chose in Step 3, say aloud, "My genius is _____ _____."

As you say the words, notice how you feel. Trust your felt sense of the rightness or wrongness of the words as a name for your genius.

Finding the Face of Genius

This exercise will help you to create your own image of the term *genius.* The list below contains English-language terms used to describe genius by those who have studied its many forms.

Step 1: Check the items that seem close to your current understanding of the term *genius.*

- ❏ Life power
- ❏ Spiritual double
- ❏ Vital energy
- ❏ Manifestation of the spirit
- ❏ Gift from God
- ❏ Spiritual vehicle
- ❏ Vital spirit
- ❏ Guardian spirit
- ❏ Higher self
- ❏ True name
- ❏ Core process
- ❏ Mystic virtue
- ❏ Essential character
- ❏ Inner form
- ❏ Divine spark
- ❏ Image of God
- ❏ Essence of life

- ❏ Unique talent
- ❏ Strong inclination
- ❏ Spirit energy
- ❏ Interior force
- ❏ Spirit guide
- ❏ Divine presence
- ❏ Guardian angel
- ❏ Positive, purposeful force
- ❏ Seed of the soul
- ❏ Basic nature
- ❏ Natural foundation
- ❏ Intrinsic power
- ❏ Special treasure
- ❏ Essential quality
- ❏ Energy of the soul
- ❏ Tutelary spirit
- ❏ Guiding star

Step 2: How would you describe the concept of genius to a friend? Use your own words and borrow from the list above.

_____

_____

_____

_____

Refuting Your Disrepute

The negative labels that people have used to describe you—your disrepute—often provide clues to your genius. Common examples of negative labels are "bossy," "loud," "shy," "unfocused," "flighty," "intense," "compulsive," and "stubborn." The most important negative labels to explore are those that hurt you and have stayed with you. You remember them because they wounded your spirit. In order to see the clues, you must ask yourself what you were trying to accomplish that was perceived as annoying or inconvenient to the person who assigned the label.

Step 1: List the negative labels that others have assigned to you.

Step 2: For each of the negative labels in Step 1, describe what you were trying to accomplish that was perceived as annoying or inconvenient to the person who assigned the label.

_____   _____

_____   _____

_____   _____

_____   _____

Step 3: Examine the list in Step 2. Look for a common denominator. For example, the items on Neil's list all had one thing in common—in each instance, he was trying to explore a pathway. Complete the sentence below by filling in the blanks (use a gerund in the first blank).

The common denominator among the items listed in Step 2 is . . .

_____ _____.

Following Your Frustration

Frustration occurs when it seems that your conscious plans or unconscious agendas are being thwarted. You feel baffled and, perhaps, useless. Frustration offers clues to your genius. Ask yourself, "What is it about me that is being frustrated?" For example, Joyce, whose genius is Digging Deeper, felt frustrated when her husband or co-workers appeared to be skating along on the surface of life and work.

Step 1: List the people or situations that have caused you frustration.

Step 2: List what you were trying to accomplish when the person or situation you listed in Step 1 caused you frustration.

_____

_____

_____

_____

_____

Step 3: Find the common denominator among all of the items listed in Step 2. Complete the sentence below by filling in the blanks (use a gerund in the first blank).

The common denominator among the items listed in Step 2 is . . .

_____ _____.

Step 4: Say it aloud. Using the two words that you chose in Step 3, say aloud, "My genius is _____ _____."

As you say the words, notice how you feel. Trust your felt sense of the rightness or wrongness of the words as a name for your genius.

Examining Your Elation

Elation that accompanies the sense of "I did it!" often arises when the intention of your genius is realized—you are successful. In order to recognize your genius within your elation, take the question you asked about your frustration but ask instead "What is it about me that is being fulfilled?"

Step 1: List situations that have resulted in elation for you.

Step 2: List what you were trying to accomplish in each of the situations you listed in Step 1.

_____

_____

_____

_____

_____

Step 3: Find the common denominator among all of the items listed in Step 2. Complete the sentence below by filling in the blanks (use a gerund in the first blank).

The common denominator among the items listed in Step 2 is . . .

_____ _____.

Step 4: Say it aloud. Using the two words that you chose in Step 3, say aloud, "My genius is _____ _____."

As you say the words, notice how you feel. Trust your felt sense of the rightness or wrongness of the words as a name for your genius.

Observing What You Offer

Every spiritual and cultural tradition that includes the concept of genius contains the idea that your genius is the gift you have been given so that you might offer it to others. When you are considering your gift, think beyond tangible items. For example, Neil gives people plane tickets, but behind that, he consistently tries to offer others the gift of new pathways to explore.

Step 1: What do you consistently attempt to give to others? It may be useful to think of specific people, groups, and circumstances.

_____

_____

_____

Step 2: What are others seeking when they come to you? It may be useful to think of specific people, groups, and circumstances. It may also be useful to ask others to help you answer this question.

_____

_____

_____

Step 3: Find the common denominator among all the items listed in Steps 1 and 2. Complete the sentence below by filling in the blank lines (use a gerund in the first blank line).

The common denominator among the items listed in Step 2 is . . .

_____ _____.

Step 4: Say it aloud. Using the two words that you chose in Step 3, say aloud, "My genius is _____ _____."

As you say the words, notice how you feel. Trust your felt sense of the rightness or wrongness of the words as a name for your genius.

Looking into Your Interests

Your genius is present in activities that you do solely for yourself, whether or not other people are involved. You can find clues to your genius in such activities by identifying the shared thread of intent among your interests. Your intent is the contribution your genius attempts to make when it is switched on.

For example, Derek, whose genius is Gathering Spirit, collects American stamps of the early 1900s because they capture the spirit of that time. He also reads many books about spirituality, looking for ideas that resonate with him. His agenda in these activities is gathering spirit.

Step 1: List activities that you enjoy solely for their own sake.

_____

_____

_____

_____

_____

Step 2: Study the list above to find the shared thread among all of the items. What is your reason for engaging in these activities? Complete the sentence below by filling in the blanks (use a gerund in the first blank).

The shared thread of intent among the items listed in Step 1 is . . .

_____ _____.

Step 3: Say it aloud. Using the two words that you chose in Step 2, say aloud, "My genius is _____ _____."

As you say the words, notice how you feel. Trust your felt sense of the rightness or wrongness of the words as a name for your genius.

Studying Your Success

This five-step exercise is intended to help you generate words that might describe your genius by examining your past successes. Many of your moments or periods of success occur when your genius is operating at full throttle, in situations when it is needed and is valued by the other people involved. This exercise will help you answer the question "What did I bring to situations in which I was most successful?"

Step 1: Tell three stories. Think about three instances in your life when you were successful, you felt good about yourself, and whatever you were doing just seemed to flow. "Successful" means success by whatever criteria you choose for defining success. "Felt good about yourself" means that you felt a sense of accomplishment and rightness about whatever you were doing. "Just seemed to flow" means that things came easily and naturally to you. These three instances can be from any period in your life. They might be about your work or hobbies, or about something you did with your family. They might be singular spontaneous events or processes that occurred over a longer period of time. The examples must meet only these three criteria:

- You were successful.

- You felt good about yourself.

- Things just seemed to flow naturally.

Describe each of the three instances in the spaces on the opposite page. When you are writing, focus on what you actually did, not on what other people did or on the circumstances surrounding the event. Do not write a description of the event so much as a description of what you did during the event. Use the word *I* frequently in describing your behavior, your thoughts, and your feelings—what you brought to the situation.

EXERCISE 10 (continued)

First story

_____

_____

_____

_____

_____

Second story

_____

_____

_____

_____

_____

Third story

_____

_____

_____

_____

_____

Step 2: Create a list of action words. Examine your three stories for words that describe actions you took. The words will most often follow the word *I*. For example, in my first story, I wrote, "I designed training programs." The word that would go on this list is *designed*. Write a word each time it appears, even if more than once.

——————————————— ——————————————— ———————————————

——————————————— ——————————————— ———————————————

——————————————— ——————————————— ———————————————

——————————————— ——————————————— ———————————————

——————————————— ——————————————— ———————————————

Step 3: Create a list of object words. Examine your three stories once again. Look for words or phrases that describe what you acted on. These words or phrases will most often follow the action words you listed in Step 2. For example, in the sentence "I designed training programs," these words would be *training programs*. Write a word each time it appears, even if more than once

If you question whether a word or phrase should go on the list, put it on the list anyway. The purpose of this exercise is to generate words that might offer clues to your genius, so do not worry about precision.

——————————————— ——————————————— ———————————————

——————————————— ——————————————— ———————————————

——————————————— ——————————————— ———————————————

——————————————— ——————————————— ———————————————

——————————————— ——————————————— ———————————————

Step 4: Choose words. In the boxes below, write the one word from the list in Step 2 and the one from the list in Step 3 that attracts you the most. Do not concern yourself with why the word attracts you; trust your intuition.

The word from Step 2 that most attracts you:	**The word or phrase from Step 3 that most attracts you:**

Step 5: Say it aloud. Using the two words that you chose in Step 4, say aloud, "My genius is _____ _____."

As you say the words, notice how you feel. Trust your felt sense of the rightness or wrongness of the words as a name for your genius.

Investigating Compelling Images

Images that compel you are potent gateways to recognizing your genius because genius lies closer to the soul, which transacts its business in images, than to the mind, which deals in words and thoughts. For example, Neil, whose genius is Exploring Pathways, enjoys looking at maps, and Joyce, whose genius is Digging Deeper, collects reproductions of pottery dug from Native American ruins.

Step 1: Think of at least three images that compel you. The images could be taken from photographs, paintings, drawings, sculpture, etc. Use the box below to describe the images in words, sketches, or whatever other means you wish. This is a four-step exercise that continues on the following pages.

Step 2: Explore the meaning of the images that you indicated in Step 1. You might explore them by answering questions such as the following. Are there people in the images with whom you identify? If so, in what way do you identify with them? What are the people doing, and why does the activity appeal to you? What do you think they are gaining from what they are doing? What are they doing that other people would appreciate? If there are no people in the images, what is it about the images that appeals to you? What do they represent? What meaning do they have for you?

_____

_____

_____

_____

_____

_____

_____

_____

Step 3: Find the common denominator among the images that you listed. Complete the sentence below by filling in the blanks (use a gerund in the first blank).

The common denominator among the images that compel me is . . .

_____ _____.

Step 4: Say it aloud. Using the words that you chose in Step 3, say aloud, "My genius is _____ _____."

As you say the words, notice how you feel. Trust your felt sense of the rightness or wrongness of the words as a name for your genius.

Creating an Image

The first two steps of this exercise are warm-ups for the steps that follow. The exercise will work best if you do not look ahead but begin Step 1 immediately.

Step 1: Draw a picture of a flower in the box below. Begin immediately, without thinking too much about it, and complete the picture in ten seconds.

Step 2: Draw a picture that represents the concept of tranquility in the box below. Begin immediately, without thinking too much about it, and complete the picture in ten seconds.

Step 3: Draw a picture of your genius in the box below. Begin immediately, without thinking too much about it, and complete the picture in ten seconds.

Step 4: Describe both the drawing in Step 3 and your process of drawing:

_____

_____

_____

Step 5: Consider whether the drawing in Step 3 and the description in Step 4 suggest a name for your genius. If they do, write the name in the blanks below (use a gerund in the first blank).

_____   _____.

Step 6: Say it aloud. Using the words that you chose in Step 5, say aloud, "My genius is _____   _____."

As you say the words, notice how you feel. Trust your felt sense of the rightness or wrongness of the words as a name for your genius.

Meeting Your Genius

In this four-step exercise, you will imagine yourself meeting your genius. Hold a serious meeting, or have fun, or both. Be imaginative. Make statements about yourself to your genius. Ask questions. Continue the dialogue elsewhere if there is not enough space here.

Step 1: Write an imaginary dialogue between you and your genius.

You: _____

Your genius: _____

You: _____

Your genius: _____

You: _____

Your genius: _____

You: _____

Your genius: _____

You (you might want to ask your genius for its name if you haven't already done so):

_____

Your genius: _____

You: _____

Your genius: _____

EXERCISE 13 *(continued)*

Step 2: Write whatever you noticed about your genius from the dialogue in Step 1.

_____

_____

_____

_____

_____

Step 3: Consider whether the dialogue in Step 1 and your response in Step 2 suggest a name for your genius. If they do, write the name below (use a gerund in the first blank).
_____ _____.

Step 4: Say it aloud. Using the words that you chose in Step 3, say aloud, "My genius is _____ _____."

As you say the words, notice how you feel. Trust your felt sense of the rightness or wrongness of the words as a name for your genius.

TO ANSWER THE QUESTION

"Is Your Genius at Work?"

EXERCISE 14

Reshaping Your Job

If your genius is not at work often enough in your current job, you might try to reshape the job. For example, Dave, whose genius is Straightening Up, spoke with his boss, explaining what he had discovered about himself and the kinds of situations in which he is most effective and satisfied. His boss reassigned him to another management job where he would have the opportunity to straighten up.

Sometimes, the solution is even simpler, and just a slight shift in responsibilities is needed.

Step 1: List the duties and responsibilities of your current job.

Step 2: For each duty or responsibility that you list in Step 1, check the box that best describes the degree to which your genius is at work when you are performing the duty or responsibility.

	Never	Seldom	Sometimes	Often	Always
_____	❏	❏	❏	❏	❏
_____	❏	❏	❏	❏	❏
_____	❏	❏	❏	❏	❏
_____	❏	❏	❏	❏	❏
_____	❏	❏	❏	❏	❏
_____	❏	❏	❏	❏	❏
_____	❏	❏	❏	❏	❏
_____	❏	❏	❏	❏	❏
_____	❏	❏	❏	❏	❏
_____	❏	❏	❏	❏	❏
_____	❏	❏	❏	❏	❏
_____	❏	❏	❏	❏	❏

Step 3: What conclusions do you draw from your responses in Step 2?

_____

_____

_____

_____

_____

Step 4: If your genius is not at work often enough in your current job, how might the job be reshaped?

_____

_____

_____

_____

_____

Step 5: What will you do with the results of this exercise? When will you do it?

_____

_____

_____

_____

_____

Checking Your Calendar

Sometimes, what we actually do at work differs greatly from what might be expected from examining a list of duties and responsibilities (as in Exercise 14). This exercise helps you look at what you actually did over the past month in order to discover whether your genius has been at work.

You will need your calendar for the past month.

Step 1: List the work activities that consumed most of your time over the past month. Be specific about the activities rather than describing general duties and responsibilities.

Step 2: For each activity you listed in Step 1, check the box that best describes the degree to which your genius was at work.

Never	Seldom	Sometimes	Often	Always
❏	❏	❏	❏	❏
❏	❏	❏	❏	❏
❏	❏	❏	❏	❏
❏	❏	❏	❏	❏
❏	❏	❏	❏	❏
❏	❏	❏	❏	❏
❏	❏	❏	❏	❏
❏	❏	❏	❏	❏
❏	❏	❏	❏	❏
❏	❏	❏	❏	❏
❏	❏	❏	❏	❏
❏	❏	❏	❏	❏

EXERCISE 15 *(continued)*

Step 3: What conclusions do you draw from your responses in Step 2?

_____

_____

_____

_____

_____

Step 4: If your genius has not been at work often enough over the past month, what can you change in the future?

_____

_____

_____

_____

_____

EXERCISE 16
How You Add Value

When you recognize your genius, you will also have the language to communicate how you add value to the work you do. This ability is invaluable when job seeking or explaining your services to potential clients.

If you have not yet recognized your genius, come back to this exercise after you have.

Step 1: Write your name for your genius.

_____

Step 2: Explain your name for your genius as you would to a potential employer or client.
For example, Dan, a manager whose genius is Charting the Course, told a prospective employer, "I excel at taking a group to its intended destination, to achieve its goals or vision." Tom, who buys, rents, and resells homes, and whose genius is Finding Jewels, told a prospective renter, "I love to find attractive houses at good prices and then provide them to people at a reasonable cost."

_____

_____

_____

_____

_____

EXERCISE 17
Allowing Your Genius to Thrive

Understanding the work conditions under which your genius thrives will help you determine the changes you might want to make in your current situation and what you need in your next situation. For example, Dave's genius, Straightening Up, thrives when he manages a situation that needs considerable improvement. Alicia, whose genius is Making It Work, does best in situations where those around her are deeply committed to their work.

If you have not yet recognized your genius, come back to this exercise after you have.

Step 1: List work situations in which your genius has thrived.

Step 2: List what it was about each situation you listed in Step 1 that allowed your genius to thrive.

_____

_____

_____

_____

_____

_____

_____

_____

_____

_____

_____

_____

Step 3: Describe what your responses in Step 2 suggest about changes you might make in your current work situation and what you need in your next one so that your genius can thrive.

_____

_____

_____

_____

_____

TO ANSWER THE QUESTION

"What Is Your Purpose?"

EXERCISE 18
Strong Emotions

Michael Azzopardi took the envelope that was handed to him. It was the beginning of a twenty-two-year path of purpose resulting from his strong feelings about the challenged and neglected children of Malta and their families.

Step 1: List situations during or about which you experienced strong emotions.

Step 2: For each of the situations listed in Step 1, note what it was about those circumstances that caused you to feel the way you did.

_____   _____

_____   _____

_____   _____

_____   _____

_____   _____

_____   _____

_____   _____

_____   _____

Step 3: Examine your responses in Step 2. Look within them for what Viktor Frankl called "a concrete assignment" for you to carry out—a need and an insight about how to meet that need. If you find such an assignment, use the space below to write one phrase or sentence that describes it. For example, Alan wrote "To create organizations composed solely of people doing their right work."

_____

_____

_____

_____

What Other People Ask of You

After Toni's divorce, she sought help from a counseling agency. Later, the people who ran the agency, recognizing her skill and empathy, asked Toni to volunteer as a counselor. She eventually formed her own company in order to fulfill her purpose: helping others identify their truth and serving the poor in spirit.

Step 1: Write several brief statements describing what people have asked of you because they saw a talent, drive, or possibility in you.

_____

_____

_____

_____

_____

_____

_____

Step 2: Examine your responses in Step 1. Look within them for what Viktor Frankl called "a concrete assignment" for you to carry out—a need and an insight about how to meet that need. If you find such an assignment, write one phrase or sentence that describes it.

_____

_____

_____

_____

_____

Unexpected Experiences and Turning Points

For Toni, the divorce, counseling, and the invitation to volunteer at the counseling center were unexpected experiences. They became turning points in her life that suggested a further turning point, the start of her business. Alan had an unexpected experience as well: his firing and subsequent six months of reflection. He too launched a new business.

Unexpected experiences are often turning points, and they also may suggest future turning points. In this three-step exercise, you will identify the important unexpected experiences and major turning points in your life in order to investigate whether they suggest your purpose and a direction for your life.

Step 1: Create a life line. Use the line on the next page to display the key unexpected experiences and turning points in your life. Many people find it valuable to use a large sheet of paper.

- Write your current age at the right end of the line.

- Place an X at the appropriate place on the line to mark each major turning point or unexpected event in your life. Label each X.

Here is an abbreviated version of Toni's life line as an example. Your life line may have few or many points marked on it.

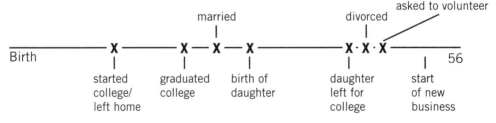

Birth

Step 2: Considering the events and turning points on your life line, can you sense a pattern? Toni, for example, saw that she had been, in her words, "programmed to be a wife and mother" and then underwent a dramatic shift in her more recent years. It was during that shift, when she was asked to counsel people in transition, that she found the most significant clue about her purpose. Alan saw his firing as an unexpected experience that was the beginning of a major turning point, which culminated in his new business.

_____

_____

_____

_____

_____

Step 3: Do the unexpected experiences and turning points in your life suggest a need and an insight about how to meet that need? If so, write one phrase or sentence that describes it.

_____

_____

_____

_____

_____

Your Suffering

Viktor Frankl believed that purpose often arose through transforming a personal tragedy into a triumph. A psychiatrist and a survivor of Nazi concentration camps, he transformed his personal tragedy into a system of therapy that focuses on finding meaning in life. While Frankl serves as an example for this exercise, avoid the temptation to compare the depth of your personal tragedies and suffering to his or to anyone else's.

Step 1: Briefly describe circumstances during which you experienced suffering.

Step 2: For each circumstance listed in Step 1, note what you learned from your experience.

_____

_____

_____

_____

_____

_____

_____

_____

_____

_____

Step 3: Examine your responses in Step 2. Look within them for what Frankl called "a concrete assignment" for you to carry out—a need and an insight about how to meet that need. If you find such an assignment, write one phrase or sentence that describes it. I imagine that Frankl would have described his assignment as "to search for meaning."

_____

_____

_____

_____

_____

EXERCISE 22
Meditation and Prayer

When you are seeking a sense of purpose, some form of prayer or meditation—quieting the mind—can be immensely valuable.

Step 1: Be quiet and alone with this page. Employ whatever means of meditation or prayer is comfortable for you: read sacred texts, recite familiar prayers, take a walk along a riverbank as Alan did, or sit on a secluded park bench.

Step 2: After you have spent what seems to you to be a sufficient amount of time at Step 1, write about your experience.

_____

_____

_____

_____

_____

_____

_____

_____

_____

_____

_____

_____

_____

_____

_____

_____

Family History

My mother wanted me to paint, and I did receive art training. As I was writing my first book, I found myself reaching back to that training. The book is a synthesis of my experience as an artist and a management consultant, an attempt to integrate artistry with all work. My experience as a practicing artist became grounding for guiding others to find the artistry in their own work. Likewise, Maya sees her history of childhood abuse as grounding for her purpose as a healer.

Step 1: Write a summary of the messages you received when you were young about the kind of work you were supposed to do as an adult.

_____

_____

_____

_____

_____

_____

Step 2: Write a summary of how those messages influenced you.

_____

_____

Step 3: Examine the messages you wrote about in Step 1. Do they suggest "a concrete assignment" for you to carry out—a need and an insight about how to meet that need? If so, write one phrase or sentence that describes the assignment.

_____

_____

_____

EXERCISE 24
Recurring Ideas

Toni is interested in alternative living arrangements for senior citizens. She also has a recurring idea about creating a worldwide network of group housing arrangements for senior citizens that would also serve as retreat centers, with the senior citizens managing and staffing the centers.

Step 1: Describe any recurring ideas you have had.

_____

_____

_____

_____

_____

_____

Step 2: Examine the ideas you described in Step 1. Do the recurring ideas described above suggest "a concrete assignment" for you to carry out—a need and an insight about how to meet that need? If so, write one sentence that describes the assignment.

_____

_____

_____

Step 3: What will you do immediately to begin acting on the assignment you described in Step 2?

_____

_____

_____

EXERCISE 25
Wouldn't It Be Great?

This exercise is intended to help you answer the question "What is your purpose?" Your purpose might also be detected in your wishes for what the world immediately around you, or at large, might become, compared to what it is.

Step 1: Complete the following statements.

In the world immediately around me,

wouldn't it be great
if _____,

and wouldn't it be great
if _____?

For the people who are served by my work (customers, clients, etc.),

wouldn't it be great
if _____,

and wouldn't it be great
if _____?

In the world at large,

wouldn't it be great
if _____,

and wouldn't it be great
if _____?

Step 2: What do your answers in Step 1 suggest about your purpose?

_____

_____

_____

_____

What Is Needed

This exercise is intended to help you answer the question "What is your purpose?" The insight that fuels purpose arrives when we see what is and then look beyond it or see it in a new way. It reaches further than the mere perception of a need; it also advocates a way to fulfill the need. This exercise will help you catalogue needs that you perceive and insights about how to meet those needs.

Step 1: Complete the following statements:

What my immediate work environment needs is_____,
and my insight about how to meet that need is_____.

What my profession or field needs is_____,
and my insight about how to meet that need is_____.

What my clients (or customers) need is_____,
and my insight about how to meet that need is_____.

What my community needs is_____,
and my insight about how to meet that need is_____.

What our nation needs is_____,
and my insight about how to meet that need is_____.

What the world needs is_____,
and my insight about how to meet that need is_____.

What our nation needs is_____,
and my insight about how to meet that need is_____.

What the world needs is_____,
and my insight about how to meet that need is_____.

Step 2: What do your answers in Step 1 suggest about your purpose?

_____

_____

_____

TO ANSWER THE QUESTION

"Is Your Genius on Purpose?"

Tendencies That Help or Hinder

You can facilitate the process of bringing the energy of your genius to your purpose. For example, if you learn optimism, you are more likely to succeed. But you can also interfere in troublesome ways. The tendencies to procrastinate, believe you are not good enough or educated enough, fear failure or success, fail to nurture yourself or find others who nurture you—all of these tendencies and many others can throw you off course.

Step 1: List tendencies of yours that will facilitate bringing the energy of your genius to your purpose.

_____

_____

_____

_____

Step 2: List tendencies of yours that may get in the way of bringing the energy of your genius to your purpose.

_____

_____

_____

_____

Step 3: What resources can you draw on to help you overcome the tendencies you listed in Step 2, for example, friends, associates, mentors, and counselors?

_____

_____

_____

Taking Responsibility

When you assume a responsible orientation, you do not blame others, luck, or fate for what you are being, doing, having, or feeling. You ask instead, "What has happened, what is the situation, how did I contribute, what is to be learned, and what shall I do next?" If you wish to adopt a responsible orientation in your life, you must move away from the victim orientation that produces blame.

Step 1: List any situation or feeling that is unpleasant for you.

Step 2: For each of the situations or feelings listed in Step 1, write a brief statement describing how you have contributed to it. Do this without blaming yourself.

_____

_____

_____

_____

_____

_____

_____

_____

_____

_____

Step 3: Explore your own internal conflict for each situation in Step 1. For example, if I don't visit Uncle Charley, I will feel guilty; if I do visit him, I will feel resentful. The conflict has everything to do with me and not much to do with Uncle Charley.

_____

_____

_____

_____

_____

_____

_____

Improving Awareness

When well developed and finely tuned, awareness stretches in many directions. It looks after your physical, intellectual, emotional, and spiritual well-being. It attends to the circumstances of your life: the people with whom you interact, the activities in which you engage, and where you live and work.

Step 1: Check the areas in which you would like to improve awareness of your well-being.

❏ **Physical:** awareness of the body, including conditions that facilitate or hinder the fulfillment of your genius and mission. For example, disease or low energy may hinder you.

❏ **Intellectual:** awareness of ideas and thoughts, including those that facilitate or hinder the fulfillment of your genius and mission. For example, thoughts of "I can't" or "I shouldn't" may hinder you.

❏ **Emotional:** awareness of feelings, including those that facilitate or hinder the fulfillment of your genius and mission. For example, optimism may facilitate, while fear, resentment, or envy may hinder.

❏ **Spiritual:** awareness of yourself as a spiritual being, connected to the divine. For example, spiritual practices may facilitate, while disavowing the spiritual aspects of your genius and purpose may hinder.

Step 2: What resources can you draw on to help you develop your awareness in the areas that you checked above? These might include, for example, friends, associates, mentors, and counselors.

_____

_____

_____

_____

_____

_____

_____

Awareness of Support

Your awareness alerts you to those aspects of your self, your life, and your work that nourish and support your genius and purpose as well as to those that do not.

Step 1: List the people in your life who now support or could support you in your attempts to fulfill your genius and mission.

_____   _____

_____   _____

_____   _____

_____   _____

_____   _____

Step 2: List the people in your life who now do not support or will not support you in your attempts to fulfill your genius and mission.

_____   _____

_____   _____

_____   _____

_____   _____

Step 3: Describe the actions suggested by your responses in Steps 1 and 2.

_____

_____

_____

_____

Finding the Courage

Courage is an indispensable part of the platform on which genius, self, and purpose come alive—the courage to act in ways that are consistent with your genius and purpose even when the future cannot be guessed, when fears about personal inadequacy, success, or failure rear up threateningly, or when your very identity seems in doubt.

Step 1: In order to remind yourself of your capacity for courage, list the times in your life when you acted courageously.

_____   _____

_____   _____

_____   _____

_____   _____

_____   _____

Step 2: List below circumstances in your current work life that will require you to be courageous.

_____   _____

_____   _____

_____   _____

_____   _____

Step 3: What resources can you draw on to help you develop and maintain the courage you need in order to meet the challenges you listed in Step 2? These might include, for example, friends, associates, mentors, and counselors.

_____

_____

_____

SUMMARIZE

Reality Check and Plan

This exercise will help you summarize all of the work you have done in this book and plan your next steps.

Step 1: If you recognize your genius, write its name below. If you have a felt sense of your genius, but not a name, describe it. If you do not yet recognize your genius, describe the next steps you will take in order to recognize and find a name for it.

_____

_____

_____

_____

_____

Step 2: If your genius is at work, congratulations! If it is not, describe what you will do next to bring your genius to work.

_____

_____

_____

_____

Step 3: If you know your purpose, describe it below. If you do not yet know your purpose, describe the next steps you will take to know it.

_____

_____

_____

_____

Step 4: If your genius is on purpose, congratulations! If it is not, describe the next steps you will take to bring your genius to your purpose.

_____

_____

_____

_____

_____

Step 5: Describe any aspects of your self that are interfering with your attempts to bring your genius to your purpose and the steps you will take to make them less troublesome.

_____

_____

_____

_____

_____

APPENDIX A
Guidelines for Guides to Genius

This book contains many guidelines for coaches, counselors, mentors, trainers, educators, therapists, and others who want to help people who are in search of their genius. The guidelines are collected here and are illustrated where possible with examples drawn from the chapters.

There are three overarching guidelines:

1. Create a space of safety for the whole person—for the physical, intellectual, emotional, and spiritual energies of the person you are helping. Recognizing a genius is often challenging, and I have the sense that many geniuses are timid or withdrawn. This is true even of the geniuses of people who seem confident. Perhaps those shy geniuses have been locked away in dark places or otherwise ignored or abused. They do not readily make their presence known unless they are made to feel safe, which is your job.

2. Be utterly relentless in pursuit of genius. View everything the person says or does as a potential clue to the genius, and respond in ways designed to help the person recognize his or her unique spirit. This guideline can be challenging for those whose training in psychology or psychiatry may lead them to analysis of motives or of past events. Such analysis is useful in a therapeutic relationship, but recognizing genius is not therapy.

The temptation most often arises when the person seeking his or her genius relates a traumatic experience, such as Maya's childhood abuse or Toni's sudden and unexpected divorce. Such experiences are, of course, the raw material of therapy. But if your purpose is to recognize genius, it is best to empathize briefly—"That's sad. I am sorry it happened to you."—and then return to the search for genius with questions such as, "How did you respond?"

The work of helping another person recognize his or her genius is guiding and facilitating rather than directing or analyzing. *Guiding* means having a sense of the territory to be crossed (described in the chapters and exercises in this book) and suggesting possible routes. *Facilitating* means making it easy for the person to cross the territory.

3. Don't let your ego get in the way of another person recognizing his or her genius. There are two common ways your ego can interfere with another person's process of recognizing his or her genius. The first way occurs when you insist that your guess about the person's genius is right. One of two things is likely to happen if you do that, and both of them are counterproductive. If you are wrong, the conversation may devolve into a dispute, squandering your credibility and distracting the person from his or her process of recognizing the genius. If you are right, you may very well rob the person of coming to his or her own conclusion. People tend to trust and keep in mind their own conclusions more than those of others, and the experience of a felt sense of rightness at the moment of recognition is crucial.

If you do make a guess and the person agrees, ask him or her to say it aloud: My genius is _____. In that way, you can check that the person has a felt sense of rightness about the name, that it is his or her conclusion and not mere acceptance of yours.

So by all means take a stab at it, pose it as a guess or a hypothesis, but do not insist. The best way to avoid letting your ego get in the way is to adopt a firm rule that you will never insist that your guess is right.

The second way your ego can interfere occurs when you try too hard to be successful. You will know that this is happening if you begin to feel frustrated or irritated with the person, or if you are working very hard and making very little progress, or if you feel as though you and the person are running in circles. Sometimes the genius or the person resists recognition. Respect that resistance. Straining against it will only make it stronger.

The best thing to do in these circumstances is take a break. Explain that sometimes the process of recognizing a genius benefits from a break in order to allow information to germinate. Taking a break will also give you an opportunity to get your need to be successful under control. Remind yourself that success is the person's responsibility; you are just there to help.

With these three overarching guidelines as backdrop, here are a few basic dos and don'ts:

1. Do know your stuff. The "stuff" I am referring to includes, at the very least,

- The conditions of the thought experiment to recognize genius (in Chapter 2)

- The ability to recognize a felt sense of the rightness of a name (also in Chapter 2)

- The approaches to searching for genius (in Chapter 3)

- The meaning of the term *genius* (in Chapter 4)

- The fields of experience in which genius is often found (in Chapter 5)

- The exercises (in the exercises chapter)

2. Do listen, reflect back, and hypothesize. Listen for clues to a genius. Tell the person what you hear that might relate to his or her genius. Make guesses about the genius, but do so sparingly.

Once again, never insist that your guess is right. Here is an example.

> *I made a guess based on what I saw and what she had told me so far. Her heart must be involved in what she does, and she was frustrated that those around her seemed not to have their hearts involved, only their minds. Your frustration is another clue to your genius. You will feel frustrated when your genius is thwarted by the circumstances or people around you.*
>
> *I said, "It sounds like your genius has something to do with bringing the heart into play. Is your genius Involving the Heart?"*
>
> *"The right word is not involving, she said, "The heart is always involved. But it is not always* engaged.*"*
>
> *One of the more satisfying aspects of helping someone recognize his or her genius is that I don't have to be right, only close, and the person will refine what I have offered. In fact, I am in danger of subverting the other person's process if I maintain that I am right.*
>
> *Francine was thoughtful for a moment, and then said, "My genius isn't Involving the Heart. It's Engaging the Heart."*
>
> *I was not sure how Francine distinguished between involving and engaging, but it doesn't matter if I understand. It only matters that she does.*

3. Do collect evidence. More often than not, the person you are helping will not naturally associate the different pieces of information he or she provides. It may be up to you to make those associations—as observations and hypotheses, not as truths. Here is an example.

> *Ann asked, "What are your hobbies, Frank?"*
>
> *"I photograph wildlife," he replied. "I like searching the woods for clues—tracking. The photography is really kind of secondary; it's proof that I found what I was looking for."*
>
> *I had another hunch. "Could your genius be something like Searching for Clues?" I asked. Frank was looking directly at me,*

and his eyes grew wide. I thought I was on to something, but I knew Frank had to arrive at his genius himself. I would explain my hunch but not try to convince him of its validity. It is crucial in these sessions to allow people to arrive at their own conclusions.

"You search for clues about wildlife in the woods. You've been searching for clues about other people's geniuses. It appears that you want others to have the gift of your clues."

4. Do interrupt. When a seemingly strong clue to a person's genius presents itself, it can be useful to capture the moment by interrupting the person. The person may be in the middle of a story, focused on the story itself, and feel surprised by or even resentful about the interruption. However, the purpose of telling the story is to recognize the genius and not to tell a story. The teller often gets so absorbed in the telling that the purpose is forgotten. So interrupt. Apologize for the interruption if you feel you must, but do interrupt. By doing so you will point out the clue while it is fresh and also remind the person why he or she is telling the story. The next time the person tells you a story, he or she will be more likely to examine the story along with you during the telling.

5. Don't get lost in the story. People usually tell really interesting stories about themselves when trying to recognize their genius. If you find yourself wanting to ask questions about the story—Did he really do that? What happened next? Were you scared?—you are lost in the story. When you become lost in the story, you are in danger of missing the genius.

6. Never insist that your guess is right. Enough said.

7. Do watch body language. When helping someone else recognize his or her genius, body language is important in two ways. First, gestures used while trying to recognize a genius are often strong clues to the genius itself, as in the following example, which also demonstrates how to make use of such gestures.

When Derek spoke of building his congregation, he repeatedly moved his hands and arms with a motion that reminded me of someone trying to get his arms around a tree trunk, almost a hugging motion. Gestures often provide clues to genius, as if the genius is expressing itself through the body. I asked Derek to perform the gesture repeatedly until he could put words to it.

Repeating the motion with his arms, he said, "Gathering. I am gathering something. In this case, gathering people."

Another man frequently repeated a gesture with his hands while speaking of his genius. The gesture involved chopping the side of his right hand into the palm of his left hand. I noticed the gesture and, on a hunch, asked him if he thought it might tell him something about his genius. He said that the gesture was an expression of his desire to "cut through" all of the information he had about his genius and arrive at a name. He eventually named his genius Cutting Through.

Body language is also important when a person is close to recognizing his or her genius. He or she often brightens noticeably, as in this example.

Francine unfolded her arms, leaned forward, and said, "I have to get right down to what matters, to the heart of things and to the heart of each person I work with. When my heart is engaged, I know that something is good and right and has to be done. This is not an intellectual knowing, and it is not exactly a feeling. It is a deep inner knowledge."

As she spoke, her hands came alive in waves and flutters. Her attitude changed. She talked about getting to the heart of things with conviction and pride. Her eyes were alight.

8. Do pay particular attention to the words the person uses. Clues to a genius are often found when the person repeats a certain word, says a particular word with strong emotion, or applies some other emphasis such as a rising or falling tone of voice. In the previous example, Francine used the word *heart* three times, each time with stronger emphasis.

9. Do notice seemingly unconnected thoughts and comments. Genius often "leaks out" rather than announcing itself with blaring trumpets. Body language is one way it leaks out, and another is through thoughts that seem to come from nowhere and "throwaways," side comments often said quietly and to no one in particular. Here is an example of an unconnected thought.

> *"I don't know. I can't get at it," she replied. "But while Frank was talking about how I connect with other people's feelings, I thought of my former career. I used to work as a nurse. I got out because it was tearing me apart."*
>
> *Ann was paying attention to a seemingly extraneous thought about her nursing career. Such thoughts are often important clues about genius.*
>
> *"How was it tearing you apart?" I asked.*
>
> *Ann suddenly looked shocked. Her face crumbled. She leaned over, hiding her face in her hands. Her shoulders shook. She was crying.*
>
> *"You just got it, didn't you?" I said to her.*
>
> *She sat up again, tears still flowing down her cheeks.*
>
> *"Yes," she replied softly, "my genius is Feeling Deeply."*

And here is an example of a side comment from Frank, whose genius is Searching for Clues.

> *"My wife often tells me, 'You don't miss a trick,'" Frank said.*
>
> *He also added, in a quiet aside to the person sitting next to him, "I don't have a clue."*
>
> *Such asides, which I call "throwaways," often are significant clues to a person's genius. I began to wonder if Frank's genius has something to do with clues.*

10. Do push, and do pull back. Perhaps the most difficult aspect of helping someone recognize his or her genius is sensing when to push the person into a deeper understanding and when to back off for a while. The need for a gentle push most often occurs when the person has adopted a name for the genius that is so general or abstract that it doesn't accurately describe his or her uniqueness—the onion needs peeling. Here is an example.

> Frank said, "What I notice about you, Ann, is that you really seem to connect with other people's emotions. You look sad when someone else is having a tough time, and you smile easily when someone else is laughing about something. When I was frustrated yesterday you seemed to understand it completely."
>
> "I do," Ann replied. "That's why I think my genius has something to do with other people."
>
> "What is your unique way of helping?" I asked.
>
> By definition, genius is an offering to other people, so saying that your genius is helping is like saying that your genius is your genius; it does not add to your understanding. The question to ask is, What is my unique offering? I wanted Ann to see that she helps others in ways that she helps herself, and that her way of helping is hers alone.

The time to back off is when you are not making progress and both you and the other person are feeling frustrated. Such frustration may indicate that the person is very close to recognizing his or her genius and is experiencing some resistance. A statement such as this one is often useful: You may be getting close to recognizing your genius and might benefit from some time out from the conscious work in order to let your unconscious bubble up.

11. Do watch for the Aha!, the felt sense of rightness. The Aha!, the felt sense of rightness, or what one person called a "buzz," can show up in a number of different ways. Sometimes it shows up as tears. Sometimes laughter. Sometimes shock. The moment when it shows up has been described as looking in the mirror, seeing yourself for the first time, and really liking what you see.

> I said, "Maybe your genius is *Taking Care* rather than *Taking Charge*."
>
> Tia is not given to overt displays of emotion, but at that moment, she began to cry.
>
> Later, she described the experience. "You talk about gut feelings!" she told me. "When you said 'Taking Care,' something just bubbled up inside me. It started somewhere in my gut and came straight up. What an emotional release! Taking Care just felt so right, and I felt so relieved to know myself in that way. It was wonderful. In that instant, I truly saw myself. I saw my own energy and power."

These moments make the work worthwhile.

APPENDIX B
Guidelines for Study Groups

I have conducted meetings, presented workshops, delivered keynotes, and given lectures about genius for groups as small as three people and as large as two hundred. In this study guide I offer the benefit of my experience to those who wish to convene a group for the purpose of helping members discover their genius.

Unless expert facilitation is available, such groups should be no larger than six to eight people. It is not essential that group members know one another well. While the people who know you well have important information about you, they may also have many preconceived notions about you, and so may have difficulty seeing you in a new way. They may also try to convince you of the validity of their perceptions about who you are rather than allowing you to go through whatever process you need to go through to recognize your genius. It is unusual in genius workshops for people to know one another well, yet people are consistently able to help one another simply by noticing one another, reporting what they notice, being uncritical, and listening. If you put a group together, invite people who can do those four things whether or not they are acquainted.

All the exercises in this book can be adapted for group use. The simplest way to do so is to have members complete an exercise individually and then discuss the results with the group. However, some exercises lend themselves to working in pairs or trios, and that should be done whenever possible. Working together on exercises provides group members with more information about one another than does working individually and then discussing results. The additional information—real-time information rather than reporting—can be used as feedback to help members recognize their genius.

For example, *Exercise 10: Telling Stories* is particularly effective when done in pairs. That exercise calls for you to write three stories about times in your life when you were successful, then to search through the stories for key words that might describe your genius. Working in a pair, one person can tell the stories aloud to the other person, who then notes the key words he or she hears. Then, the person who was listening and making notes can report what he or she heard to the person who was telling the stories, and together they can look for the genius. The advantage is that another person has partnered with you in the search for your genius and likely provided information that you would not have noticed.

When you are trying to help another person, notice the person's process as he or she tries to find a name. Look for signs of frustration and ask, "What is it about you that is being frustrated right now?" Also look for signs that his or her genius is getting in the way. If the person says, "I've got it!" and then starts looking elsewhere for it, does his or her genius have something to do with considering alternatives? Don't get so caught up in the content of the stories that you fail to notice what is happening right in front of you.

Trying to recognize a genius is like putting together a five-hundred-piece jigsaw puzzle. When two people are trying to help each other, it is like trying to cooperate to put two five-hundred-piece jigsaw puzzles together simultaneously. Work on them one at a time. Take turns. If you seem to be getting nowhere with one of them, go to the other for a while. If you seem to be getting nowhere with either puzzle, it is time for a break.

Remember, you are the only expert on your own genius. Only you know your true intent, even if you are struggling to uncover it. Resist any temptation to convince another person that you know the correct name for his or her genius. If you are right, the other person will discover it too. If you are wrong, you will lead him or her down a fruitless path. If another person attempts to convince you that he or she knows the correct name for your genius, but you don't experience a felt sense of the rightness of that name, ask the person to stop trying to convince you.

When you are part of a group, your primary tasks are to

- Recognize your genius

- Notice others and report what you notice

- Be uncritical

- Listen

- Never insist that your guess about someone else's genius is right

Remember also to look for the physical response that indicates the felt sense of rightness of the name for someone's genius. The response may be a smile, tears, a look of shock or surprise, or some other reaction. When people are trying to help one another name their genius, it is important that they look at one another.

Remind one another often of the eight conditions of the thought experiment to name your genius. They are described in detail in Chapter 2. Here is a summary.

1. **You do have a genius.**
2. **You have only one genius.**
3. **Your genius has been with you for your entire life.**
4. **Your genius is natural and spontaneous, and a source of success.**
5. **Your genius is a positive force.**
6. **Your genius is not what you wish it would be; it is what it is.**
7. **Your name for your genius should contain one gerund and one noun.**
8. **Your name for your genius will be unique.**

There are two other important advantages to working in a group. First, one test of the rightness of your name for your genius is to announce it to the group. Say to the group, "My genius is _____." How does it feel to say that out loud? If you don't feel anything at all, then you probably have not yet found your genius. There should be some emotional energy. Sometimes the energy is nervousness and reluctance, but more often it is the pure joy of significant self-discovery.

Watch and listen to others as they announce their names. You will soon be able to tell when a person has found the right name. For example, if the person is shaking his or her head from side to side when speaking to the group, the name is probably wrong. If the person says the sentence, then shrugs as if to say "No big deal," the name is probably wrong. If the person lights up, smiles, or seems pleased just after saying the sentence, the name is probably right.

Remember that the decision about the correctness of a name for your genius, and of others' names for theirs, is not a matter of intellectual judgment. It is a matter of the felt sense of whether the name fits. Physical reactions when announcing the name to others are indicators of the felt sense.

The second major advantage of working with a group is the opportunity to use name tags. Whenever you think you might have a new name for your genius, write that new name on a name tag and wear it. This will encourage attention—from both you and others—to your genius. It will also allow you to metaphorically "try on" a name, wear it for a while, and see if it feels right in the way that some clothing feels right.

Change your name tag as often as a new name comes to mind. As you look at it you may notice yourself thinking "That's not right." If so, trust that impulse and keep searching for a name.

When you arrive at the name that seems right, you will feel pleased about writing it down, sticking it on, and announcing it to the group.

APPENDIX C
Resources for Further Reading

To my knowledge, there are no books in print other than this one aimed specifically at helping you recognize your genius. However, there are many books that treat the concept of genius, one or more of the four key questions, or other topics in this book. Some of the best are listed below.

Bloch, D. L., and Richmond, L. J. *SoulWork: Finding the Work You Love, Loving the Work You Have.* Mountain View, CA: Davies-Black Publishing, 1998.

Boldt, Laurence. *Zen and the Art of Making a Living: A Practical Guide to Creative Career Design.* New York: Penguin, 1993.

Bolles, R. N., and Bolles, M. E. *What Color Is Your Parachute? 2005: A Practical Manual for Job Changers.* Berkeley, CA: Ten Speed Press, 2004.

Chopra, D. *The Seven Spiritual Laws of Success: A Practical Guide to the Fulfillment of Your Dreams.* San Rafael, CA: Amber-Allen, 1994.

Covey, S. *The 7 Habits of Highly Effective People.* New York: Fireside, 1989.

Csikszentmihalyi, M. *Flow: The Psychology of Optimal Experience.* New York: HarperCollins, 1990.

Dunning, D. *What's Your Type of Career? Unlock the Secrets of Your Personality to Find Your Perfect Career Path.* Mountain View, CA: Davies-Black Publishing, 2001.

Dyer, W. *The Power of Intention: Learning to Co-Create Your World Your Way.* Carlsbad, CA: Hay House, 2004.

Fox, M. *The Reinvention of Work: New Vision of Livelihood for Our Time.* San Francisco: HarperSanFrancisco, 1994.

Frankl, V. *Man's Search for Meaning.* New York: Simon & Schuster, 1984.

Gendlin, E. *Focusing.* New York: Bantam, 1982

Hall, D. *Life Work.* Boston: Beacon Press, 1993.

Harkness, H. *The Career Chase: Taking Creative Control in a Chaotic Age.* Mountain View, CA: Davies-Black Publishing, 1997.

Hillman, J. *The Soul's Code: In Search of Character and Calling.* New York: Random House, 1996.

Jeffers, S. *Feel the Fear and Do It Anyway.* New York: Fawcett Columbine, 1987.

Jones, M. *Creating an Imaginative Life.* Berkeley: Conari Press, 1995.

Keen, S. *Hymns to an Unknown God: Awakening the Spirit in Everyday Life.* New York: Bantam Books, 1994.

Kiersey, D, and Bates, M. *Please Understand Me: Character and Temperament Types.* Del Mar, CA: Prometheus Nemesis, 1984.

Leider, R J. *The Power of Purpose: Creating Meaning in Your Life and Work.* San Francisco: Berrett-Koehler, 1997.

Leider, R J., and Shapiro, D. *Repacking Your Bags: Lighten Your Load for the Rest of your Life.* San Francisco: Berrett-Koehler, 1994.

Moore, T. *Care of the Soul: A Guide for Cultivating Depth and Sacredness in Everyday Life.* New York: HarperCollins, 1992.

Myers, Isabel B., with Myers, Peter B. *Gifts Differing: Understanding Personality Type.* Mountain View, CA: Davies-Black Publishing, 1995.

Nachmanovitch, S. *Free Play: Improvisation in Life and Art.* New York: Tarcher Putnam, 1990.

Richards, D. *Artful Work: Awakening Joy, Meaning, and Commitment in the Workplace.* San Francisco: Berrett-Koehler, 1995.

Seligman, M. *Learned Optimism: How to Change Your Mind and Your Life.* New York: Pocket Books, 1990.

Simonson, P. *Career Compass: Navigating Your Career Strategically in the New Century.* Mountain View, CA: Davies-Black Publishing, 1997.

Somé, M. *The Healing Wisdom of Africa: Finding Life Purpose Through Nature, Ritual, and Community.* New York: Tarcher Putnam, 1998.

Warren, R. *The Purpose-Driven Life: What on Earth Am I Here For?* Grand Rapids, MI: Zondervan, 2002.

Whyte, D. *The Heart Aroused: Poetry and the Preservation of the Soul in Corporate America.* New York: Currency Doubleday, 1994.

Williamson, M. *A Return to Love: Reflections on the Principles of "A Course in Miracles."* New York: HarperCollins, 1992.

Zukav, G. *The Seat of the Soul.* New York: Fireside, 1989.

NOTES

CHAPTER 2

1. Plato, *Cratylus*. Retrieved [[Date?]] from http://classics.mit.edu/Plato/cratylus.html.

2. Eugene Gendlin, *Focusing* (New York: Bantam, 1982), p. 32.

3. Gendlin, *Focusing*, pp. 33–40.

4. Werner Heisenberg, *Physics and Beyond: Encounters and Conversations* (New York: Harper Torchbooks, 1972), p. 77.

5. Heisenberg, *Physics and Beyond*, p. 77.

6. Heisenberg, *Physics and Beyond,* p. 78.

CHAPTER 3

1. I first heard these lines from people affiliated with the Gestalt Institute of Cleveland. None of those people knows the source. Apparently, the author is anonymous. The last four lines are sometimes attributed to Marilyn Ferguson.

2. Marianne Williamson, *A Return to Love: Reflections on the Principles of "A Course in Miracles"* (New York: HarperCollins, 1996).

CHAPTER 4

1. James Hillman, *The Soul's Code* (New York: Random House, 1996), p. 7.

2. Hillman, *The Soul's Code,* p. 11.

3. Plato, *The Republic*, translation by H. D. P. Lee. Retrieved from http://www.classics.und.ac.za/Er%20Narrative.txt.

4. *The Catholic Encyclopedia*. Retrieved from http://www.newadvent.org/cathen/07049c.htm.

5. Hillman, *The Soul's Code,* p. 7.

6. Vera Schwarcz, *Bridge Across Broken Time: Chinese and Jewish Cultural Memory* (New Haven, CT: Yale University Press, 1998).

7. *New American Standard Bible*, 1 Corinthians 12:7 and 1 Peter 4:10.

8. "Attaining True Simcha!" Retrieved from http://simcha.ilovetorah.com.

9. Lao Tzu, *Tao Te Ching*, translation by C. Ganson, verse 38. Retrieved from http://www.geocities.com/Athens/Delphi/7395/arctao1.html.

10. Malidoma Somé, *The Healing Wisdom of Africa* (New York: Jeremy P. Tarcher/Putnam, 1998), p. 33.

11. Somé, *The Healing Wisdom of Africa*, pp. 102–103.

12. Deepak Chopra, *The Seven Spiritual Laws of Success* (San Rafael, CA: Amber-Allen, 1994), p. 98.

13. John Pemberton III, "Divination in Sub-Saharan Africa." Retrieved from http://www.metmuseum.org/explore/oracle/essay4.html.

14. Lao Tzu, *Tao Te Ching*, verse 38.

15. S. N. Tandon, "Dharma—Its Definition and Universal Application." Retrieved from http://www.vri.dhamma.org/research/95sem/sem9505c.html.

16. *New American Standard Bible*, Psalm 91:10–11.

17. Somé, *The Healing Wisdom of Africa*, pp. 33–34.

18. William Blake, *The Portable Blake*, edited by Alfred Kazin (New York: Viking Penguin, 1946), p. 176.

19. Ananda Coomaraswamy, *Christian and Oriental Philosophy of Art* (New York: Dover, 1956), p. 38.

20. James Hillman, *The Soul's Code* (New York: Random House, 1996), p. 27.

CHAPTER 5

1. Hans Selye, Stress Without Distress (New York: Signet, 1974), p. 76.

CHAPTER 7

1. Marion Zimmer Bradley, *The Mists of Avalon* (New York: Ballantine Books, 1984).

2. Laurence Boldt, *Zen and the Art of Making a Living* (New York: Penguin, 1993), p. 161.

3. Deepak Chopra, *The Seven Spiritual Laws of Success* (San Rafael, CA: Amber-Allen, 1994), p. 100.

4. James Redfield, *The Celestine Prophecy* (New York: Warner, 1993), p. 141.

5. Thomas Moore, *Care of the Soul* (New York: HarperCollins, 1992), p. 181.

6. Matthew Fox, *The Reinvention of Work* (San Francisco: HarperSanFrancisco, 1994), p. 106.

7. Richard J. Leider, *The Power of Purpose* (San Francisco: Berrett-Koehler), p. 8.

8. Redfield, *The Celestine Prophecy*, p. 146.

9. Stephen Covey, *The 7 Habits of Highly Effective People* (New York: Fireside, 1989), p. 128.

10. Leider, *The Power of Purpose*, p. 3.

11. Rick Warren, *The Purpose-Driven Life: What on Earth Am I Here For?* (Grand Rapids, MI: Zondervan, 2002), p. 20.

12. Victor Frankl, *Man's Search for Meaning* (New York: Simon & Schuster, 1984), p. 113.

13. Williamson, *A Return to Love* (New York: Harper Collins, 1992), p. 192.

14. Leider, *The Power of Purpose*, p. 1.

15. Sam Keen, *Hymns to an Unknown God* (New York: Bantam Books, 1994), p. 278.

16. Michael Azzopardi, "A Story of Something Beautiful." The story was sent to me by Lewis Portelli, Monsignor Azzopardi's friend.

17. Lewis Portelli, "Mgr. Michael Azzopardi: An Appreciation by Lewis Portelli," *The Sunday Times* (Malta), May 31, 1987.

18. Portelli, "Mgr. Michael Azzopardi."

19. Frankl, *Man's Search for Meaning*, p. 116.

20. Zalman Schachter-Shalomi and Ronald S. Miller, *From Aging to Saging: A Profound New Vision of Growing Older* (New York: Warner Books, 1995), pp. 2–3.

21. Redfield, *The Celestine Prophecy*, p. 138.

22. Redfield, *The Celestine Prophecy*, p. 139.

CHAPTER 8

1. Matthew 25:14–30, *The Holy Bible: New Revised Standard Version* (Iowa Falls, IA: World Bible Publishers, 1989), pp. 26–27.

2. Rainer Maria Rilke, *Letters to a Young Poet, Letter Four,* Retrieved from http://www.nyx.net/~kbanker/chautauqua/rilke.htm.

3. Victor Frankl, *Man's Search for Meaning* (New York: Simon & Schuster, 1984), p. 116.

4. Eleanor Roosevelt, *This Is My Story* (New York: Harper & Brothers, 1937).

INDEX

your intuition and, 67–68;
uniqueness of, 22–23; warnings
regarding, 39–40; words used
in, 40, 118–119
need, 88–90, 160
negative labels, 60
noticing: description of, 23;
exercise for, 122–123
not noticing what you do, 29–31,
35–36

observing what you offer, 63–64, 128

peeling the onion analogy, 31–34,
120–121
Plato, 17, 19–20, 47–49, 52–53
pneuma, 49
Portelli, James, 91
positive force, 21, 78–79
prana, 49
prayer, 95–96, 156
productivity, 3–4
purpose: case studies of, 88–94,
102–103; clues to, 92–98;
description of, 5, 53; discovering
of, 86–87; focus in life and, 88;
fulfilling of, 88; genius and,
91–92; insight that fuels, 90–91;
meaning of, 86–88; names for,
86; need and, 88–90; outward
direction of, 87–88; pursuing of,
87–88, 171–172; sense of, 85;
support for, 165; tendencies that
help or hinder, 100, 162

reality check, 168–169
recognizing your genius: Aha!
experience after, 24–25, 30,
69, 178–179; associating, 23;
benefits of, 2–4; blinding flash
associated with, 70, 72, 74; case
studies of, 74–82; ego's effect on,
172–175, 56, 63, 127; elusive-
ness of, 13–14; examining your
elation, 56, 63, 127; in fields of
past experience. *See* fields of past
experience; following your
frustration, 56, 61–63, 126;
investigating compelling images,
56, 67, 134–135; looking
beneath the surface, 23; looking
into your interests, 64–66, 129;
moment of, 70–71; naming,
15–17; noticing. *See* noticing;
not noticing what you do,
29–31, 35–36; observing what
you offer, 63–64, 128; peeling
the onion analogy for, 31–34,
120–121; processes for, 55–57;
pushing during, 178; refuting
your disrepute, 55, 60–61, 125;
studying your success, 56, 64,
130–133; weaknesses as clues
to, 60
recurring ideas, 97–98, 158
Redfield, James, 86
refuting your disrepute, 55, 60–61,
125
relationship, 16–17
reshaping of job, 83, 142–143
responsibility, 103–106, 163
revelation, 96
rightness of name, 71, 184
Rilke, Rainer Maria, 101–102

safety space, 171
Saint Jerome, 48
satisfaction, 3–4
self: awareness as aspect of, 107–109,
164; conceptualization of, 6,
100–101; as a covering, 100;
definition of, 100; information
gathering about, 29–39
self-confidence, 3
self-knowledge, 3
Selye, Hans, 61–62
sense of direction, 3
sense of identity, 2–3
service to others, 50–51, 54
shared thread of intent, 36–39, 65
Somé, Malidoma, 44, 50
spiritual calling, 88
strong emotions, 93, 150
study groups, 181–184
studying your success, 56, 64, 130–133
suffering, 94–95, 155